The Seven Spirits of God that Every Christian Needs

By

Prophetess Mary J. Ogenaarekhua

Endorsement

"The Seven Spirits of God that Every Christian Needs" by Prophetess Mary O. *draws you closer to God and helps you to understand how to operate in His ways and by these Spirits. You will also learn what it truly means to put on Christ 'the miraculous workings' of God through His Seven Spirits. As I was reading this book, the Spirit of God ministered to me, He brought me to repentance and His anointing touched my life. I hope that you will be as blessed by the Lord as I was when I was spending time with Him in the pages of this book. Thank You Lord for Your blessings through this book."*

—Lynne Garbinsky,
Chief Operations Officer,
THGP/MJM, Atlanta, Georgia.

Dedication

As with all my books, I dedicate this book to my heavenly Father, my Lord Jesus Christ and my Lord the Holy Spirit. LORD God, You gave me the words to write in this book and I thank You for it because without Your teachings, I will not have anything to write. I also thank You for teaching me about Your **Seven Spirits** and also for giving me the grace to write what You taught me as it is written in **Psalm 68:11**:

> "**The Lord gave the word**: great was the company of those that published it."

LORD God, may this book bring You much glory and may You use it to bring Your children and those who desire to know You closer to You.

I also dedicate this book to all those who want to walk more intimately with God by knowing Him through His **Seven Spirits**. I hope that this book is a major tool in your efforts to know God and to draw closer to Him.

The Seven Spirits of God
that Every Christians Needs

Unless otherwise indicated, all scriptures are
quoted from the King James Version of the Bible.

Published by: To His Glory Publishing Company, Inc.
463 Dogwood Drive, NW
Lilburn, GA 30047
(770) 458-7947
www.tohisglorypublishing.com

This Book is available at:
Amazon.com, BarnesandNoble.com, Booksamillion.com,
UK, EU, Canada, Australia, etc.

Also, see the Order Form at the back of this book or call/email
below to order this book.

(770) 458-7947
www.tohisglorypublishing.com
Email: tohisglorypublishing@yahoo.com

ISBN: 978-1-942724-07-0

Table of Contents

Preface

This book is designed to help us know God the Father and the Lord Jesus by His **Seven Spirits. The truth is that, every one of us needs to operate in all of God's Seven Spirits.** The Lord Jesus told us that **God is a Spirit** and that those who worship Him, must worship Him in spirit and in truth. According to Him, these are the type of worshipers that God the Father seeks— **John 4:23-24**:

> "But the hour cometh, and now is, when the <u>true worshippers shall worship the Father in spirit and in truth</u>: for the Father seeketh such to worship him. 24 **God is a Spirit: and they that worship him <u>must</u> worship him in spirit and in truth.**"

Some people might not be aware that God has **Seven Spirits** but most people know **the Lord Holy Spirit. Therefore, this book is designed to help us know His other Spirits that are <u>in the</u> Holy Spirit.**

—**Prophetess Mary J. Ogenaarekhua**

Acknowledgements

Heavenly Father, I acknowledge the gift of a Scribe that you have given me and I thank You for fulfilling Your Word to me through Your Son, my Lord Jesus Christ that:

> **"Every scribe which is instructed unto the kingdom of heaven** is like unto a man that is an <u>householder,</u> **which bringeth forth out of his <u>treasure</u> things new and old"** (Matthew 13:52).

Thank you Lynne Garbinsky for helping me proofread, edit and layout this book. You are a steadfast soldier and may the Lord bless you beyond your imagination.

Chapter 1
We Are Essentially Spirit Beings

Definition of a Spirit

A **spirit** is defined as a supernatural being or the essence of a being such as **our human spirits** and **the Holy Spirit**. It is the sentient or perceptive part of a person. To the Christian, a **spirit** means the **breath of God** that is the life giving source in every human being — **Genesis 2:7**:

> "And the LORD God formed man of the dust of the ground, and **breathed into his nostrils the <u>breath of life</u>;** and man became **a living soul**."

God made man to have three (3) parts: **spirit, soul** and **body** because God Himself is made up of three parts. This is why when the **spirit** (breath of God) departs from a person, the **body** dies and the person can no longer live on earth. **Even people who do not believe that God exists, live by God's breath because His breath is the life in every living soul.** The day that the breath of life (God's spirit) departs, the person dies. That person's **soul** cannot remain in the body; it has to vacate it. **The <u>spirit</u> goes back to God and the <u>soul</u> can now stand independently before God for its actions while it was in the body.**

Biblical Account of God's Seven Spirits

Some of us have not given great thought to the fact that **God has Seven Spirits**. We have learned about some of these Spirits individually without knowing that they are collectively known as **God's Seven Spirits. We first learned that God has Seven Spirits in the prophecy concerning the Messiah in the Book of Isaiah.** The prophecy which God gave to Israel over 500 years before the Lord Jesus was born states that, the **Seven Spirits** of God will rest upon the **Messiah** when He comes — **Isaiah 11:1-5**:

"And there shall come forth a rod out of the stem of Jesse, and a Branch shall grow out of his roots: 2 And **the spirit of the LORD** shall rest upon him, **the spirit of wisdom** and **understanding**, **the spirit of counsel** and **might**, the **spirit of knowledge** and of **the fear of the LORD**; 3 **And shall make him of quick understanding in the fear of the LORD:** and he shall not judge after the sight of his eyes, neither reprove after the hearing of his ears:

4 But **with righteousness shall he judge the poor, and reprove with equity (balance) for the meek of the earth: and he shall smite the earth with the rod of his mouth, and with the breath of his lips shall he slay the wicked.** 5 And righteousness shall be the girdle of his loins, and faithfulness the girdle of his reins."

In the above scripture, we can clearly see that God has **Seven Spirits** and it also tells us what these Spirits will do for the Messiah when He comes into the world. **He will carry the Spirit of the Lord, He will have great understanding, He will have great wisdom, He will have great counsel and might. He will judge fairly and no one can persuade Him to deviate from the truth. He will be gentle, meek, reprove fairly and walk in the fear of the Lord.**

He will also be stern and will punish those that need to be punished because He will wear righteousness as a belt (sash). **This means that He will gird Himself with righteousness and faithfulness.** Since His loins are girded with righteousness and faithfulness, no one will doubt or second guess Him when He judges something. **In essence, it means that these Spirits will help the Messiah to accomplish His ministry or the Call of God upon His life.**

The Lord Jesus Confirmed Having the Seven Spirits of God

When the Lord Jesus came into the world, these **Seven**

Spirits were truly at work in Him. For example, when the devil came against Him after 40 days of fasting saying to Him, "If you be the Son of God..." do this and that, He defeated the devil by being faithful to use the **Spirit of the Lord, the Spirit of Knowledge, the Spirit of Wisdom, the Spirit of Understanding, the Spirit of Might, the Spirit of Counsel and the Spirit of the Fear of the Lord.**

As a result, the Lord Jesus **Succeeded** where Adam had **failed** because the devil tried the same tactics on Him that he used on Eve (and Adam through Eve) by questioning God's Word and truthfulness. Having seen this tactic of the devil, you have to understand that it takes the **Seven Spirits of God** to keep you throughout your life time and especially when the devil comes against you. **If the Lord Jesus needed them to keep Him, you better believe that you also need them to keep you.**

In His letter to the churches in the Book of Revelation, the Lord Jesus confirmed that the **Seven Spirits of God** dwelt in Him — **Revelation 3:1-2**:

> "And unto the angel of the church in Sardis write; **These things saith <u>he that hath the Seven Spirits of God</u>, and the Seven stars;** I know thy works, that thou hast a name that thou livest, and art dead. 2 Be watchful, and strengthen the things which remain, that are ready to die: for I have not found thy works perfect before God."

This message was to the church in Sardis and not to a group of unbelievers. This was probably a large church with lots of members, funds and great prestige. When the society in those days looked at its outward appearance, they may have thought that this was a very successful church. **Today, you can see similar churches in operation; where the ministers preach the Word of God just as a means to their personal ends. They do not stay faithful to the Spirit of the Word but twist (corrupt) the Word to mean what they want.**

You see some of them on TV manipulate their congregations as they tell them to put their 'Faith Seed' on a **credit card** thereby getting the whole congregation into credit card debt. **These ministers then turn around and pray for debt cancellation for the members!** God watches these types of behaviors from heaven and He cries for His children. Therefore, do not manipulate the Word of God or use it for personal gain.

The Seven Spirits Are Before the Throne of God

The Apostle John tells us that these **Seven Spirits** are before the throne of God in heaven — **Revelation 1:4-5**:

> "John to the <u>Seven churches</u> which are in Asia: Grace be unto you, and peace, **from him which is, and which was, and which is to come; and from <u>the Seven Spirits which are before his throne</u>;** 5 And from Jesus Christ, who is the faithful witness, and the first begotten of the dead, and the prince of the kings of the earth. Unto him that loved us, and washed us from our sins in his own blood."

The Lord Jesus went back to heaven after accomplishing the mission that God the Father sent Him on concerning our redemption. In other words, after He made a way for us to be reconciled to God, He went back to heaven. As a result, these **Seven Spirits** are now before the throne of God and the Lord Jesus Christ who is the faithful witness; the first begotten from the dead and the Prince of the kings of the earth.

Furthermore, John tells us about the <u>functions</u> of the **Seven Spirits** in heaven. They burn as <u>Seven Lamps of fire before the throne of God</u> — **Revelation 4:4-5**:

> "And round about the throne were four and twenty seats: and upon the seats I saw four and twenty elders sitting, clothed in white raiment; and they had on their heads crowns of gold. 5 <u>And out of the throne proceeded lightnings and thunderings and voices</u>:

and **there were <u>Seven lamps of fire burning before the throne, which are the Seven Spirits of God</u>.**"

Because these Spirits burn like a lamp, when the Lord Jesus said to us, **"Ye are the light of the world,"** He knew what He was talking about because He <u>carried</u> the **Seven Spirits** that light up everywhere He is. **These Spirits light up His Life and His Life is now in us; it makes us Light to the world!** The Lord allowed me to see visions of how the 'Born Again' Christians look as the 'New Creations' in heaven.

In these visions, when you see the 'New Creations' in heaven, they <u>illuminate</u> and <u>radiate light</u> just like the Lord Jesus. There is a trail of light with every step they take because He is the very Life in them and they are in Him. At first glance, you think that the person you are looking at, is the Lord Jesus coming towards you. It is only when you see the person's face closely that you realize that it is not Him! Without looking at the face, the profile is that of the Lord Jesus with His regal walk and flowing robe. This is the reason why the Bible tells us that:

> "For as many of you as have been <u>baptized into Christ</u> **have put on Christ**" (Galatians 3:27).

What God did for us and what He gave us in Christ is beyond our human comprehension. It is why the Word of God says in **1 Corinthians 2:9-10** that:

> "**...Eye hath not seen, nor ear heard, neither have entered into the heart of man, the things which God hath prepared for them that love him.** 10 But God hath revealed them unto us by his Spirit: for the Spirit searcheth all things, yea, the deep things of God."

Truly, what God did for us in Christ Jesus is amazing. **He actually reproduced His Son in us who believe in Him!** This why the Bible also says that we are the children of God in **Galatians 3:26**:

"For ye are all the <u>children of God</u> by faith in Christ Jesus."

It is in the millennial reign of Christ that the people who will be on earth will look at the 'New Creation' and wonder amongst themselves saying, **"Who are these people?"** just as we wonder about angels today! The reason for this is because the 'New Creation' will be God's **'Ruling Elected Class of Beings.'** They are the **fulfillment in Christ Jesus** of what He set out to create in **Genesis 1:26** when He said:

> **"...Let us make man in our <u>image</u>, after our <u>likeness</u>:** and **let them have <u>dominion</u> over** the fish of the sea, and over the fowl of the air, and over the cattle, and **all the earth**, and over every creeping thing that creepeth upon the earth **(rule the earth)."**

The 'New Creation' is the generation that God the Father created for His Son to reign and rule with Him. It is why we must <u>be conformed to the image of Christ</u>. What God did is that, He created this whole world and gave it as a gift to His Son; all of us included. Therefore, when you leave the earth and you <u>do not</u> have or <u>are not in</u> His Son, then <u>you are not</u> **the specimen** that He set out to create in **Genesis 1:26**.

At the end of time, all those that are <u>not in Christ</u> will only be fit for destruction. According to God, they are bad crops and because God is a farmer, He planted many seeds with the hope of reaping good crops. **As any farmer does, He knew that some of the seeds which He planted will not turn out as good crops because of free will, so He made arrangement to have them destroyed.** This explains why the Lord will say to some people, **"Get away from me; I never knew you"** even though, they were in the church and some of them were preaching His Word every Sunday.

The reason for rejecting them will be because <u>they never allowed God to form His character in them</u>; **they never allowed Him to conform them to the likeness or image of Christ.** We must all meet God's criteria when the Lord Jesus comes back. Anyone who claims to be a Christian and does not measure up, is not going back with Him. **Before He left, the Lord told us who He was coming back for; that man or woman who is after God's likeness** (character) **and has no blemish, spot or wrinkle!**

It is only the Lord who knows how to <u>prepare</u> His bride. **Therefore, He makes us individually ready by ironing out the wrinkles and removing the spots in our character.** From what He showed me in a vision, He puts a <u>white wedding gown</u> on every one of us (His Bride) and the whiteness of the gown represents His righteousness that He gave us. He then, places us on a pedestal while He works on us to remove the spots and wrinkles in us. **He takes the time to remove every single thing from our lives that makes us unclean.** This preparation of the Bride takes years and in the end, He puts <u>a royal sash of dominion</u> across her chest!

You cannot imagine what it will be like when the Bride (every believer) **comes to rule and reign with Christ in His Millennial Reign!** Right now on earth, what the world calls <u>royal and regal</u> does not compare to the Lord's Bride in the royal and regal department. **Until you see the Lord and His Bride, no one on earth has seen true royalty or a regal monarch.** We all need to fulfill our own calling and be conformed to Christ so that God's gift to us will make people wonder about us (the true royals) for all eternity.

The Seven Spirits as the Eyes of God

In **Revelation 5:4-7**, the Apostle John tells us that the **Seven Spirits of God** are actually God's eyes. He saw the Lamb of God sitting upon the throne with seven horns of authority and the **Seven Spirits of God:**

> "And I wept much, because no man was found worthy to open and to read the book, neither to look thereon. 5 And one of the elders saith unto me, Weep not: behold, the Lion of the tribe of Juda, the Root of

David, hath prevailed to open the book, and to loose the Seven seals thereof.

6 **And I beheld, and, lo, in the midst of the throne and of the four beasts, and in the midst of the elders, stood a Lamb as it had been slain, <u>having Seven horns and Seven eyes, which are the Seven Spirits of God</u> sent forth into all the earth.** 7 And he came and took the book out of the right hand of him that sat upon the throne."

The Function of the Seven Eyes on Earth

God sends the **Seven Spirits** into all parts of the world to record everything that happens on earth and they report it all back to God. In other words, God sends His eyes over all the earth to see what everyone is doing and they go throughout the earth to see what is going on. **There is nothing that we do that escapes them because, they are All-seeing; they are not hindered by light or darkness.**

There is nothing secret that they cannot see and report back to God to let Him know those who do things that please Him and those who are doing the works of the devil. They let Him know those who are putting their trust in Him and need His help or intervention. This is because God wants to show up strong to defend and save all who call upon Him and who depend on Him for help — **2 Chronicles 16:9**:

> "**For <u>the eyes of the LORD run to and fro throughout the whole earth</u>**, to shew himself strong in the behalf of them whose heart is perfect toward him."

Yes, these eyes record what happens on earth and report back to heaven! **On the Day of Judgment when 'The Books of Our Works' are opened, they will give the record that they kept of all our works or activities while we were earth.** <u>What we learn from this is that these eyes follow us everywhere to see and record what we are doing</u>. Therefore, when you think that you are doing something in secret and that no one can see you, know that these eyes follow you and they record everything that you are doing.

We are also told in **Zechariah 4:10**, that these **Seven Spirits** besides going all over the earth to see and record what everyone is doing, **also help us to build or do what God has commanded us to do**. We see this in the case of Zerubbabel as he was rebuilding the walls of Jerusalem. The **Seven Spirits** gave him wisdom and grace to help him along with his fellow workers in order to get the job done:

> "For who hath despised the day of small things? for they shall rejoice, and **shall see the plummet in the hand of Zerubbabel** with **those Seven; they are the eyes of the LORD, which run to and fro through the whole earth.**"

The MSG translation reads:

> "Does anyone dare despise this day of small beginnings? **They'll change their tune when they see Zerubbabel setting the last stone in place!**"

God's Commandment to His Eyes

God is awesome in His power and abilities. As a result, He can sit on His throne in heaven and **send His eyes out to search and record** everything for Him. We also learn that God gives commandment to His eyes to check out peoples' spiritual behavior — **Jeremiah 5:1-31**:

> "**Run ye to and fro through the streets of Jerusalem,** and **see** now, and **know,** and **seek** in the broad places thereof, if ye can find a man, if there be any that executeth judgment, that seeketh the truth; and I will pardon it... 29 Shall I not visit for these things? saith the LORD: shall not my soul be avenged on such a nation as this?
>
> 30 A wonderful and horrible thing is committed in the land; 31 The prophets prophesy falsely, and the

priests bear rule by their means; **and my people love to have it so:** and what will ye do in the end thereof?"

From the following commandment, we read that God's eyes went all around Jerusalem and **they could not find even one person that was crying out for righteousness.** Therefore, God drove the children of Israel away from the land.

God's Eyes Determine What the Wicked Get

We are told in **Jeremiah 32:19** that God's eyes are open to all we do:

> "Great in counsel, and mighty in work: **for thine eyes are open upon all the ways of the sons of men:** to give every one according to his ways, and according to the fruit of his doings."

When you do something wicked to someone, it is the eyes of God that see what you have done and report it to God. **As a judgment, God sends a 'more wicked' person than you to repay you for your wickedness.** Also, when you willfully sin against Him, His eyes report it to Him and He brings His judgment against you when you do not repent.

For example, when Solomon sinned against Him, He stirred up <u>two kings</u> to go to war against Solomon because of His righteous requirements which Solomon knew and willfully ignored. King Solomon chose to ignore God's commandment not to marry foreign women because they might turn him into a pagan worshiper **—1 Kings 11:9-24**:

> "**And the LORD became angry with Solomon because his heart had turned from the LORD God of Israel, who had appeared to him twice.** *10* God had given him commands about this. [He told him] <u>not to follow</u> <u>other gods</u>. **But Solomon did not obey God's command.** *11* The LORD told Solomon, "Because this is your attitude and you have no respect for my promises or my laws that I commanded you to keep,

I will certainly tear the kingdom away from you. I will give it to one of your servants.

12 But I will not do it in your lifetime because of your father David. I will tear it away from the hands of your son. 13 However, I will not tear the whole kingdom away from you. <u>I will give your son one tribe for my servant David's sake and for the sake of Jerusalem,</u> [the city] that I chose." **14 The LORD raised up Hadad the Edomite as a rival to Solomon.** Hadad was from the Edomite royal family...

23 **God also raised up Rezon, son of Eliada, as a rival to Solomon.** Rezon fled from his master, King Hadadezer of Zobah, 24 after David killed the men of Zobah. Rezon gathered men and became the leader of a troop of warriors."

Although He deferred His judgment against Solomon while Solomon was still alive, God's anger was <u>not appeased</u>. **Therefore, He promised Jeroboam 10 of the 12 tribes of Israel while Solomon was still alive!** God promised to leave Solomon's son (Rehoboam) with only the tribe of Benjamin along with the tribe of Judah that was already under Solomon. **After Solomon's death, God immediately brought His judgement against the house of Solomon by <u>inspiring Jeroboam to leave Egypt</u> and come back to Israel.** God chose him as His **instrument of judgment** against the house of Solomon as we see in **2 Chronicles 10:2-16**:

"And it came to pass, when Jeroboam the son of Nebat, who was in Egypt, whither he had fled from the presence of Solomon the king, heard it, that Jeroboam returned out of Egypt 3 <u>And they sent and called him. So Jeroboam and all Israel came and spake to Rehoboam, saying,</u> 4 **Thy father made our yoke grievous: now therefore ease thou somewhat the grievous servitude of thy father, and his heavy yoke that he put upon us, and we will serve thee...**

4 And answered them <u>after the advice of the young men</u>, saying, My father made your yoke heavy, but I will add thereto: my father chastised you with whips, but I will chastise you with scorpions. *15* **So the king hearkened not unto the people: for the cause was of God, that the LORD might perform his word, which he spake by the hand of Ahijah the Shilonite to Jeroboam the son of Nebat.**

16 And when all Israel saw that the king would not hearken unto them, <u>the people answered the king, saying,</u> **What portion have we in David? and we have none inheritance in the son of Jesse: every man to your tents, O Israel: and now, David, see to thine own house.** <u>So all Israel went to their tents.</u>"

Every time someone does something that God hates, His eyes report it to Him. Remember the interesting conversation He had with Abraham on His way to verify the report that He heard about Sodom and Gomorrah in **Genesis 18:17-21**?:

"And the LORD said, **Shall I hide from Abraham that thing which I do;** *18* Seeing that Abraham shall surely become a great and mighty nation, and all the nations of the earth shall be blessed in him...? *20* And the LORD said, <u>Because the cry of Sodom and Gomorrah is great, and because their sin is very grievous;</u> *21* **<u>I will go down now, and see</u>** whether they have done altogether according to the cry of it, which is come unto me; <u>and if not, I will know.</u>"

God physically walked to Sodom and Gomorrah to verify what His eyes had already reported to Him —all the men in the cities were wicked! When it came to Sodom, Abraham bargained with God to spare the city for the sake of those who are righteous in the city. This was because Abraham knew that **God's righteous nature will not allow Him to destroy the righteous with the wicked.**

Abraham bargained with God to spare the city for the sake of at least **fifty righteous souls** that might be in the city and Abraham eventually reduced the number of possible righteous souls in the city to **ten**. Abraham stopped at **ten** because he thought that for sure, there would be at least **ten righteous souls** in Sodom but God could only find **Lot**. Therefore, He sent His angels to bring **Lot** and his family out of Sodom.

We have to assume that there was not one righteous person in Gomorrah because God destroyed it without anyone coming out of it. In the same manner, God's eyes looked all over Jerusalem and saw that no one cared about being righteous. As a result, God brought His judgment against Jerusalem when the people did not repent.

The Guiding Eye of the Lord

God told us about His Guiding **Eye** in **Psalm 32:8-9**:

> "I will instruct thee and teach thee in the way which thou shalt go: **I will guide thee with mine eye.** 9 Be ye not as the horse, or as the mule, which have no understanding: whose mouth must be held in with bit and bridle, lest they come near unto thee."

Now that we know that God has **Seven Spirits** and also know that part of the functions of the **Seven Spirits** is to act as His eyes, we now need to address each one of the **Seven Spirits** in detail. In the next chapter, I will begin with the <u>first</u> of the **Seven Spirits** which is called **the Spirit of the Lord.**

Chapter 2
Understanding the Spirit of the Lord

The **Holy Spirit** is called the **Spirit of the Lord** and most of us have read about Him beginning from **Genesis 1:1-2** when He hovered over the frozen deep — the earth:

> "In the beginning God created the heaven and the earth. 2 And the earth was without form, and void; and <u>darkness was upon the face of the deep</u>. And the **Spirit of God** moved upon the face of the waters."

In the beginning we are introduced to God by His Word and we <u>assumed</u> that **God was alone in His existence.** This is because we read in **Genesis 1:3-11** that, "God said, God said…"

> "**And God said,** Let there be light: and there was light. 4 And God saw the light, that it was good: and God divided the light from the darkness. 5 And God called the light Day, and the darkness he called Night. And the evening and the morning were the first day.
>
> 6 **And God said,** Let there be a firmament in the midst of the waters, and let it divide the waters from the waters… 9 **And God said,** Let the waters under the heaven be gathered together unto one place, and let the dry land appear: and it was so… 11 **And God said,** Let the earth bring forth grass, the herb yielding seed, and the fruit tree yielding fruit after his kind, whose seed is in itself, upon the earth: and it was so."

In **Genesis 1:26-27**, God <u>shatters our assumption</u> that **He was alone in existence** when we see Him saying, "**Let Us.**" If you are like me, upon coming across the sentence, "Let Us," the first question that comes to mind is, "**Who is God talking to when He said, "Let Us," I thought He is One?**"

> "And God said, **Let <u>us</u> make man in our image, after our likeness:** and **let them have dominion** over the

fish of the sea, and over the fowl of the air, and over the cattle, and over all the earth, and over every creeping thing that creepeth upon the earth. 27 So **God created man in his own image**, in the **image of God** created he him; male and female created he them."

Later, we learned that the **Holy Spirit** is included in **God the Father's** statement of, "**Let Us.**" Meaning that, God spoke in the plural form of Himself; **thereby telling us that He is not alone in existence.** By His revelation, we now know that it was a conversation between **God the Father, His Word** (Jesus) and **His Spirit**; the Holy Spirit. These are the three aspects of **our God.**

The Holy Spirit's Involvement in Creation
We learn from the above scripture that God was speaking **His desire** out loud. **After He spoke the Word (Jesus), His Spirit reached out into the earth and used the Word** (Jesus) **to create a clay cast from the dust of the earth.** Then, **God the Father breathed into the clay cast** and it became **a living Soul!**

In other words, God the Father verbalized the specimen of the man He wants and His Spirit accomplished His desire by using His Words to form a man out of the dust of the earth. God the Father then breathed His Spirit into the man and Adam became a living Soul. **From this, it is clear that God first created man with His Word that He spoke before His Spirit formed the man from clay!**

It is also now clear to us that it takes the **Word** and **Holy Spirit** to bring about whatever **God the Father** says. We call them the **Godhead** or **Trinity**. If you are blessed to see **God the Father, God the Son** (Jesus) and **God the Holy Spirit** together, you will notice that they are three different personalities but still One God! **They have one voice, one thought and they act as one.**

My Vision of the Majesty on High as He Creates

Our God is a creating God and He created the heavens, the earth and all that is in them. Most of us wonder how God actually goes about the business of creation:

"Once God the Father gave me a vision of Himself as the <u>Majesty on High</u>; decked out in glory and arrayed in beauty and *He gave me a demonstration of how He creates.*

I watched as He stepped forward, stretched forth His Right Hand, spoke (made a decree; His Word), and He watched as what He decreed came into existence. He then inspects it and nods His head with a smile of satisfaction before stepping forward to make another decree.

It was obvious that when He stretched forth His hand and speaks, His Spirit and His Word actually go to create what He spoke. Therefore, God the Father, His Word (Jesus) and His Spirit were <u>all</u> involved in creation."

The Activating Power of the Spirit of God

The Lord Jesus **was** and **still is**, the **Word of God** but it takes the **Holy Spirit** to **activate** the **Word** and bring it to pass! This is why the Bible says in **Hebrews 1:1-2**, that Jesus Christ created all things. Yes, the **Holy Spirit** activates every **Word** (Jesus) that God speaks and makes it happen just as God said. **This is how the Lord Jesus became the Creator of all things before He became a human being** — God's Son:

"God, who at sundry times and in divers manners spake in time past unto the fathers by the prophets, 2 Hath in these last days spoken unto us by his Son, whom he hath appointed heir of all things, **by whom also he made the worlds.**"

Until the Lord Jesus became a human being, He was in existence as the **Word** that God speaks <u>activated</u> by the **Holy Spirit**. Today, we agree with the written Word that the Lord

Jesus created everything and that there is nothing that He did not create. As we just saw, the reason is because God creates with His Word and His Spirit so by being the Word of God, the Lord Jesus created all things.

Also, the Apostle John **confirms** that **the Lord Jesus is the Word of God** and **that He is also the God who created all things** in **John 1:1-3**:

> "**In the beginning was the Word, and the Word was with God, and the Word was God.** 2 The same was in the beginning with God. 3 **All things were made by him; and without him was not anything made that was made.**"

So, God the Father created all things by the Word that He spoke. The **Holy Spirit** took the **Word; "Let there be"** which was **Jesus**, and He made what the Father said happen. **As a result, it takes the <u>Holy Spirit</u> and the <u>Word (Jesus)</u> to get things accomplished.**

The Actions of the Word and the Holy Spirit after Adam Sinned

When Adam and Eve sinned against God, He sent them His **Word** by <u>the working</u> the **Holy Spirit** in the Garden in Eden. This is why we read that the **Voice** (Word) of God was walking in the Garden in **Genesis 3:6-21**. **This a display of the power of the Holy Spirit because it made the Word of God to walk:**

> "And when the woman saw that the tree was good for food, and that it was pleasant to the eyes, and a tree to be desired to make one wise, she took of the fruit thereof, and did eat, and gave also unto her husband with her; and he did eat. 7 <u>And the eyes of them both were opened, and they knew that they were naked; and they sewed fig leaves together, and made themselves aprons.</u>

8 **And they heard the <u>voice</u>** *(Word)* **of the LORD God <u>walking</u> in the garden in the cool of the day**: and Adam and his wife hid themselves from the presence of the LORD God amongst the trees of the garden…*21* Unto Adam also and to his wife did the LORD God make <u>coats of skins</u> *(from the Lamb He killed)*, and clothed them."

In His mercy, God **killed a Lamb in the Garden of Eden** and **He used its skin and blood to cover them and their sin.** He then taught Adam how to use the blood of bulls and goats to cover their sins annually as we saw in the history of the offerings of **Cain** and **Abel**. All the generations from Adam to Abraham offered the blood of animals to God to appease God for all their sins.

The Word of God Became Flesh by the Power of His Spirit

In order to manifest **the Lamb that He killed in the Garden of Eden in the lives of all of Adam's descendants** (all human beings), **God spoke His Word into the womb of a young girl in Nazareth named Mary. This Word incubated by the Power of the Holy Spirit in Mary's womb and came out 9 months later as a baby called Jesus!**

God nurtured this baby until He was <u>old enough</u> to house His **Holy Spirit. God's desire was fulfilled at the baptism of the Lord Jesus when God's Holy Spirit came down from heaven and <u>indwelled</u> Him.** In other words, God the Father by His Spirit was able to put His Word into a human body and that body (Jesus) walked on earth until **the Holy Spirit** came and dwelt in Him. In this <u>one man (His Word in a human body)</u>, **God the Father** and His **Holy Spirit** <u>dwelt</u> here on earth for three and a half years!

The reason God did this was because He desired a better <u>offering</u> or <u>sacrifice</u> that will forever deal with the <u>problem</u>

of sin in His creation. This is why it is recorded first in **Psalm 40:6-8** and then in **Hebrews 10:4-7** that, before His coming to earth, the Lord Jesus declared in the spirit realm that **God the Father** has **prepared a body for Him** and that He was coming into the world to do God's will:

> "Sacrifice and offering thou didst not desire; mine ears hast thou opened: burnt offering and sin offering hast thou not required. 7 **Then said I, Lo, I come: in the volume of the book it is written of me, 8 I delight to do thy will, O my God**: yea, thy law is within my heart" (Psalm 40:6-8).

And in **Hebrews 10:4-7**:

> "For it is not possible that the blood of bulls and of goats should take away sins. 5 Wherefore when he cometh into the world, he saith, Sacrifice and offering thou wouldest not, but a body hast thou prepared me: 6 In burnt offerings and sacrifices for sin thou hast had no pleasure. 7 **Then said I, Lo, I come (in the volume of the book it is written of me,)** to do thy will, O God."

The scriptures above, show us **the Lord Jesus talking as the Word of God** before He came to the earth. **Since He came to the earth in human form, God's Word now has a human body that contains both God the Father Himself and His Spirit.** What God did is an example of how we as human beings record our words or voice in a CD or a voice recorder but **because our God is awesome and powerful, He was able by His Spirit to put His Word in a human body instead of in an object like a CD**!

Remember that when God made Adam, He simply **molded clay, breathed into it** and **that clay became a human being** or a **living Soul** but with the Lord Jesus, He took His creative ability much further than clay. **He decided that the 'Last Adam' (Jesus) will be from Himself; His Word!**

34

God the Father and His Son have One Spirit

The Lord Jesus and the Holy Spirit both dwell in God the Father. In other words, the Spirit of the Father is the Spirit of the Son; they are one. This is the reason why when the disciple Philip said in **John 14:8-12,** "Show us the Father and it will suffice us," the Lord Jesus answered him saying, "Have I been with you so long and you still do not know Me?" **What Philip did not know was that when you see the Lord Jesus, you see the Father because He is not separate from His Father**; they are one.

Even today, all three (the Father, the Word and the Holy Spirit) still come together to make things happen. God the Father and the Son are sitting on their throne in heaven but the **Holy Spirit** is the one that is here on earth with us just as the Lord said in **John 14:16-17**:

> "And I will pray the Father, and he shall give you another Comforter, that he may abide with you forever; 17 Even **the Spirit of truth**; whom the world cannot receive, because it seeth him not, neither knoweth him: <u>but ye know him</u>; **for he dwelleth with you, and shall be in you.**"

This is true of all who are Born Again and are Spirit-filled; He is **with us** and **in us** as the Lord said. **It is He who brings us the fullness of the Godhead because the Spirit of God is God and the Spirit of God's Word is also God.** Again, He is the Spirit of the Father and the Spirit of the Son. **This is why the Holy Spirit is called the Spirit of Christ and the Spirit of the Father.** He makes us one with them in the fulfillment of the Lord Jesus' prayer in **John 17:21-22** that:

> "**That they all** (*believers*) **may be one; as thou, Father, art in me, and I in thee, that they also may be one in us:** that the world may believe that thou hast sent me. 22 And the glory (*the Holy Spirit*) which thou gavest me I have given them; that they may be one, even as we are one."

As we see from the scripture above, the Lord prayed to the Father about us being one with Him and the Father by the working of the Holy Spirit. Now that the Holy Spirit is living in us, **it is in essence the fullness of the Godhead** *(the Father, the Son and the Holy Spirit)* **that is dwelling in us.**

My Vision of the Godhead

This knowledge concerning God, His Word and His Spirit should help us to understand that the **Godhead** is not divided and that as a matter of fact, <u>they are one</u> in essence and unity. As a result, they function in unison because it is still <u>the one and same God</u>. **It is not complicated at all for God to function using His own Word** (Jesus) **and His own Spirit. When you are privileged to see the three of them together in Counsel, you will see that although only <u>one voice comes forth</u>, all three of them are actually saying the same thing to you!**

It is one of the most amazing sights that I have ever seen; the three of them speaking with the same (one) voice at the same time! It was truly awesome. In one of my books titled: *Experiencing the Depths of the Holy Spirit, pages 22-23*, I related this encounter with the Godhead and below is an excerpt:

> *"I was in a church service one day and the devil decided to scare me by distorting the face of someone sitting near me. He made the person's face to elongate and his ears to enlarge. As the person's ears began to expand and contract, I decided that I was going to defy what I was seeing and instead confess the Word of God in 2 **Corinthians 5:7** that says, "We walk by faith and not by sight." As I continued to make this confession, God opened heaven to me and I saw a vision of the **Godhead**.*
>
> *In this vision, I ran to them **(the Father, the Son and the Holy Spirit)** in tears crying but when I opened my mouth to launch my complaint about what the devil was doing to me, I heard <u>a voice</u> saying, '**Do not even mention his name for I will show him how much he must suffer for what he has done to my children.**' I stood perplexed before them as*

the words were being spoken to me because all three of them **seemed** *to be speaking and I could not pin-point which one of them was actually the one speaking. I became determined to discover who was speaking among the three of them.*

It was one of the most hilarious spiritual experiences that I have had because, **God the Father, God the Son** *and* **God the Holy Spirit** *were all trying not to burst into laughter as they watched me seriously determine to find out who was speaking among them by checking out each of their mouths as I was hearing the voice! It was some years later that the Lord reminded me of the encounter and how they thought it so funny that I was determined to solve the mystery of the* **Godhead**.

Due to the ignorance I displayed in the vision above concerning the **Godhead**, *you can now understand why the Lord had to teach me about who He is and about the* **Godhead**. *As a result of the spiritual discernment gifts that He has now given me, I frequently see God the Father and the Lord Jesus in visions and dreams individually and sometimes together.*

I sometimes see **God the Holy Spirit** *by Himself also, but once I saw* **God the Father** *and* **God the Holy Spirit** *together in a night vision. Remember that I am only able to see these spiritual visions by the* <u>aid</u> *of the* **Holy Spirit** *because I am in Christ, because* **Christ is in God and Christ is God's Word**. *As God Himself puts it, 'a person and his word are one.' Therefore, all three of the Persons of the* **Godhead** *are always involved in an activity."*

For a detailed discussion of this encounter, see the book that I referenced above. It is the Person of the **Holy Spirit** that uses God's Word (Jesus) to produce whatever **God the Father says.**

The Holy Spirit is the Part of the Godhead that Changes Form

Remember that God said in **Malachi 3:6**, "I am the Lord, I change not?" Therefore, **God the Father** does not change; He remains the same. **Also, the Lord Jesus does not change in essence**; He remains God's Word. Today, the Lord Jesus can appear to you as a different person each time yet, He remains the person housing God's Word. The **Holy Spirit** is different because **He is the part of God that goes and does whatever God the Father wants done and as a result, He is the part of the Godhead that <u>changes forms</u>.**

He can be **a person,** He can be **fire,** He can **flow like oil,** He can **multiply Himself** on several different people at the same time, and He can **become anything** in order to accomplish God's plans and purposes. We see Him as **a mighty rushing wind** and as **cloven tongues of fire** in **Acts 2:1-4**:

> "And when the day of Pentecost was fully come, they were all with one accord in one place. 2 And suddenly there came a sound from heaven as of **a rushing mighty wind, and it filled all the house where they were sitting.** 3 And **there appeared unto them cloven tongues like as of fire, and it sat upon each of them.** 4 And **they were all filled with the Holy Ghost,** and began to speak as the Spirit gave them utterance."

From the above scripture, we see Him doing three things at the same time. He is the **fire on their heads, different tongues** in their mouths while **filling them with Himself** at the same time!

He is the Breath of God in Man

As we saw in the **definition of Spirit,** God breathed His Spirit into Adam and he became a living Soul - **Genesis 2:7**:

> "And the LORD God formed man of the dust of the ground, and breathed into his nostrils **the breath of life;** and man became a **living soul.**"

This is why every human being has the breath of God in them and when this breath departs from a person, we say that the person is dead and if they do not bury the dead body, it will begin to stink. **When a person dies, the person's spirit returns to God who gave it.** The **soul** is the part of a person that gets judged because it is where a person's **earthly consciousness resides**. It is where we **touch, see, hear, taste, smell** or where our five senses dwell and as the Lord Jesus said, **it is where what defiles a person comes from**:

> "Not that which goeth into the mouth defileth a man; but that which cometh out of the mouth, this defileth a man...*17* Do not ye yet understand, that whatsoever entereth in at the mouth goeth into the belly, and is cast out into the draught? *18* **But those things which proceed out of the mouth come forth from the heart; and they defile the man.**
>
> *19* <u>For out of the heart proceed</u> **evil thoughts, murders, adulteries, fornications, thefts, false witness, blasphemies:** *20* **These are the things which defile a man**: but to eat with unwashen hands defileth not a man" (Matthew 15:11-20).

These things listed in the above scripture, are some of the things that the soul will be judged for because it is where they occurred in the person. It is where we house our emotions and plan our actions. Therefore, when a person is about to do something that is wrong, the Spirit through the soul gives the person a warning or puts a check in the person not to follow through with the wrong action. If the person overrides the check, he or she will be held accountable before God if the person does not repent.

All the souls that did wrong things on earth and who refused to accept the forgiveness that Christ purchased for them on the Cross, will go to hell to await judgment at the Judgement Seat of Christ. **Our soul is who we really are** because, we are in three parts consisting of a **spirit, soul** and **body**. At death, every soul that received the Lord Jesus as his or her Savior, goes to heaven to wait for its glorified body while those who did not accept the Lord Jesus as their Savior, go to hell to wait for further punishment after judgement.

Also, the **soul** can recognize the danger of death and as a result, the soul and the **spirit** are very sensitive to danger and are quick to eject when they know that the **body** is about to become **uninhabitable**. Therefore, having experienced death, I surmise that when you hear that somebody had been stabbed to death, the person is usually killed by the first stab. This is because the spirit and the soul vacate the person as the knife is at the point of making contact with the body. **It is a very quick occurrence because Christ took the sting** (pain) **out of death for all mankind.** In other words, the **spirit** and **soul** know when death is being unleashed against the body and they leave before the person can feel the pain of death.

As a result, if the murderer keeps stabbing his victim, that victim's soul will be above him looking down at the body being stabbed repeatedly without feeling anything. This is because the essence (soul) of the victim is no longer in the body being stabbed because the body being stabbed repeatedly is now nothing but a shell. The spirit returns to God because it was His 'loaned breath' to us and the soul can either go to heaven if it was saved by the blood of Jesus or to hell for its wickedness to await God's judgment.

That is why the Lord Jesus said that we should not be afraid of the people who can kill the body and after that they cannot do anything more in **Luke 12:4-5**:

> "And I say unto you my friends, **Be not afraid of them that kill the body, and after that have no more that they can do.** 5 But I will forewarn you whom ye shall fear: **Fear him, which after he hath killed hath power to cast into hell; yea, I say unto you, Fear him.**"

In my experience, the **soul** and the **spirit** are so sensitive that they know when a deadly blow or fall is coming and before it hits the body, they are out of it. **This is why I did not feel the pain of the impact of the fall that killed me. Instead, I heard a loud explosion but I felt no pain!**

The reason we do not feel the pain of death is because **as the 'Last Adam,'** the Lord Jesus gave us the breath of God and He took the 'sting of death' away from us. This is why, after the Lord Jesus rose from the dead, He **breathed** on the disciples and He told them that the **'breath'** is the **Holy Spirit — John 20:22**:

> "And when he had said this, **he breathed on them,** and saith unto them, **Receive ye the Holy Ghost.**"

Just as God breathed into the clay and it became a living soul, so the Lord breathed on the disciples and gave them life. Truly, anyone who does not know Jesus is essentially a **'walking dead.'** I know this because, during the time that I was physically dead, **I spent the first night looking for anyone who was alive; meaning, someone that had flesh on his or her skin. The reason for this was because as I looked at the people on their beds, I was shocked to see that everyone was just a skeleton without any flesh on.**

I mean, everyone in all the houses was just a skeleton on a bed and I was determined to find a normal looking human being but I could not find one in the entire town. At this time, I had no idea that I was born a Christian but was being raised by my paternal grandparents who were Muslims and as a result, Islam was all I knew.

From my experience, when you are dead, you know that something has happened to you as you see your body lying on the ground but being dead is not what you think happened to you. This is because you feel 100% better than you have ever felt and you can suddenly see what everyone in the whole town or city is doing as you look at the houses. Also, you are able to see beyond the doors, windows and roofs of houses so, although I was the one who was physically dead, I thought that everyone in the town had died and I was sad about it.

Later, the **Lord informed me that what I saw were people who were 'spiritually dead' because the saving Grace; <u>eternal life</u> which the Lord gives is not in them.** This is why He said to the man that wanted to go bury his father before becoming His disciple to, "Let the dead bury their dead" in **Luke 9:59-60**:

> "And he said unto another, Follow me. But he said, <u>Lord, suffer me first to go and bury my father</u>. *60* Jesus said unto him, **Let the dead bury their dead: but go thou and preach the kingdom of God.**"

Therefore, if you are alive today and you are not Born Again to belong to the Lord Jesus, you might be walking around thinking you are alive but to God, you are dead; you are the 'walking dead.' <u>The reason for this is because, the day Adam sinned against God, He died spiritually.</u> **In other words, the <u>Life of God</u>** (being spiritually connected to God) **departed from Him**; he became spiritually dead. **As a result of this spiritual death, <u>all the seed in Adam</u>; the generations that came from him** (the human race), **inherited this spiritual death. It is the reason why we needed a Savior; the Lord Jesus.**

He is the Source of Our New Birth

The **Lord Holy Spirit** is God's Life Giving Spirit to every human being. The Lord Jesus is the only one that gives us this New Birth (Eternal life) <u>through the Holy Spirit</u> so that **we can be spiritually alive and connected to God again**. It was also why He breathed on the disciples after His Resurrection. He breathed on them and on us through the Holy Spirit, the life of God which we lost in Adam.

The **Holy Spirit** is the difference between a Born Again Christian and someone who does not know or belong to the Lord. <u>I also saw this difference firsthand in a vision:</u>

> *<u>Right after being Born Again, I was still going to night clubs to dance and party with my unsaved friends</u>. My excuse was*

that the Lord never told me not to dance or have fun because I was now Born Again. I kept going out with my unsaved friends and the Lord decided to take a drastic action with me concerning this. **One night, as I was on the dance floor in a night club and the Lord suddenly opened my spiritual eyes to see where I was and the spiritual conditions of the people I was dancing with.**

As I looked around me, it seemed as if someone dropped me into the midst of dancing 'living skeletons!' I was shocked to see that I was the only 'regular' looking human being among these dancing 'living skeletons' without any human flesh and it scared me so much that I ran out of the club. *This was the day that I stopped going to night clubs after being Born Again and it was how the Lord delivered me from going out with my unsaved friends. He knew that I loved to dance but He wanted me to know the 'true nature' of those that I was going dancing with."*

The Holy Spirit is the Water of God

The **Lord Holy Spirit** is the **Spiritual Living Water** that quenches everyone's thirst. We see this in **John 7:37-39**:

"In the last day, that great day of the feast, Jesus stood and cried, saying, **If any man thirst, let him come unto me, and drink.** *38* He that believeth on me, as the scripture hath said, **out of his belly shall flow rivers of living water.** *39* (**But this spake he of the Spirit, which they that believe on him should receive: for the Holy Ghost was not yet given;** because that Jesus was not yet glorified)."

As the Living Water of God, the **Holy Spirit** has the ability to satisfy a human thirst like nothing can. People thirst for all kinds of things in life: **love, jobs, money, fame, prestige, respect, family, houses, friends, material things** and a slew of other things. The truth is that none of these things can satisfy those who seek them. **Actually, they create greed for** more and more of these things while amplifying the huge vacuum in them that only God can fill.

We see the Lord Jesus talking about this ability of the Living Water of God to quench the human thirst when He was talking to <u>the woman at the well</u> in **John 4:10-15. He told her that whoever drinks the water from the well** (representing the well of worldly material things) **will thirst again but whoever drinks of the water that He gives, shall never thirst.** Again, this is because the Lord Jesus is the only one who can give us God's Living Water that satisfies every thirst:

> "Jesus answered and said unto her, **If thou knewest the gift of God, and who it is that saith to thee, Give me to drink; thou wouldest have asked of him, and he would have given thee <u>living water</u>.** 11 The woman saith unto him, Sir, thou hast nothing to draw with, and the well is deep: from whence then hast thou that living water? 12 Art thou greater than our father Jacob, which gave us the well, and drank thereof himself, and his children, and his cattle?
>
> 13 Jesus answered and said unto her, **Whosoever drinketh of this water shall thirst again:** 14 **But whosoever drinketh of the water that I shall give him <u>shall never thirst</u>; but the water that I shall give him shall be in him <u>a well of water springing up into everlasting life</u>.** 15 The woman saith unto him, Sir, give me this water, that I thirst not, neither come hither to draw."

This is one of the most beautiful experiences of the Born Again Christian. **When you are filled with the Holy Spirit, and as you get closer to God, the things that people are willing to die and kill to possess in life become less important to you.** As you continue to grow in the knowledge of the Lord, the loud vacuum that has been screaming throughout your life to be filled and that you tried to fill with material things, disappears; you feel content in life! At this point, you can see clearly that those who are running around trying to fill their fleshly desires, are truly lost.

As for you, every time you get into the presence of the Lord in prayer or worship, you are refreshed, renewed and content because He is everything that you have ever longed for. The Lord is aware of this feeling that we all have when He is around us and that when it is time for Him to leave, we do not want Him to go because we do not want our satisfaction to end. **As for me, there was a time that I tried to grab His leg when I realized that He was about to leave and He knew it because right before I reached for His leg, He immediately placed a huge distance between me and Him so that I could not grab His leg! When He did this, we were now standing across the room from each other and I let out a loud cry as He turned into a very bright light and was gone.**

The Holy Spirit is the Wind of God

The Lord Holy Spirit is the Wind of God as the Lord Jesus informed Nicodemus in **John 3:3-8**:

> "Jesus answered and said unto him, **Verily, verily, I say unto thee, Except a man be born again, he cannot see the kingdom of God.** 4 Nicodemus saith unto him, How can a man be born when he is old? can he enter the second time into his mother's womb, and be born? 5 **Jesus answered, Verily, verily, I say unto thee, Except a man be born of <u>water</u> and of <u>the Spirit</u>, he cannot enter into the kingdom of God.**
>
> 6 <u>That which is born of the flesh is flesh; and that which is born of the Spirit is spirit</u>. 7 Marvel not that I said unto thee, **Ye must be born again.** 8 **The wind bloweth where it listeth, and thou hearest the sound thereof, but canst not tell whence it cometh, and whither it goeth: <u>so is every one that is born of the Spirit</u>.**"

We also saw the **Lord Holy Spirit** as a **Mighty rushing Wind** blowing into the room where the disciples were gathered together 40 days after the **Resurrection** and **Ascension** of the Lord Jesus — **Acts 2:1-2**:

> "And when the day of Pentecost was fully come, they were all with one accord in one place. 2 **And suddenly there came a sound from heaven as of a rushing mighty wind, and it filled all the house where they were sitting.**"

The Holy Spirit is the Anointing

As the Anointing, the **Holy Spirit** used to come upon the heads of the Old Testament prophets and they would begin to prophesy. When they asked Pater what was going on with them as they were speaking in "other tongues," he said that it was a fulfillment of the prophecy in **Joel 2:28-31**:

> "**And it shall come to pass afterward, that I will pour out my spirit upon all flesh; and your sons and your daughters shall prophesy, your old men shall dream dreams, your young men shall see visions:** 29 And also upon the servants and upon the handmaids in those days will I pour out my spirit. 30 **And I will shew wonders in the heavens and in the earth, blood, and fire, and pillars of smoke.** 31 **The sun shall be turned into darkness, and the moon into blood,** before the great and the terrible day of the LORD come."

The **Lord Holy Spirit** is the one that gives us God's heavenly language when He fills us up. He also brings about the fulfillment of God's prophecies through the prophets. God gives the **Holy Spirit** to people so that they can prophesy, have dreams, see visions and flow in the ability to interpret dreams and visions. It is true that unbelievers have dreams and see visions from God, but they usually do not have the ability to interpret them or get their godly meaning.

He gives them dreams and visions to warn them about imminent danger and to prick their conscious to discourage them from doing something that will harm them. For most unbelievers, visions and dreams are the primary ways that God can reach them since they do not read the Bible, go to church or watch Christian programs.

My vision of the Holy Spirit as the Anointing

"In this vision, the Holy Spirit was in the shape of a person that was made of liquid oil. He let me see how as the Anointing (oil), He was pouring Himself out upon the earth from heaven. I watched Him in awe as He continued to pour Himself out upon the earth without diminishing in size. The whole earth was almost half full with Him as oil but His size never changed even though He was gushing out as the Anointing upon the earth."

The Holy Spirit is the Gift of God to All Believers

Because the **Lord Holy Spirit** is transferable, He can be made a **Gift** by the Lord Jesus to new believers. **It is the Holy Spirit that reveals God the Father and the Lord Jesus to us.** All we learn and receive from God is through Him. He can be worshipped just like **God the Father** and **God the Son.** The **Holy Spirit** is the **Glory** that God the Father gave to His Son (Jesus) and the Lord Jesus gave the same **Glory** to all those who believe in Him. He said so in **John 17:21-23**:

> "That they all may be one; as thou, Father, art in me, and I in thee, that they also may be one in us: that the world may believe that thou hast sent me. 22 **And the glory which thou gavest me I have given them; that they may be one, even as we are one:** 23 I in them, and thou in me, that they may be made perfect in one; and that the world may know that thou hast sent me, and hast loved them, as thou hast loved me."

This is why when we get Born Again, we receive the **baptism of the Holy Spirit** as God's **Gift** to us. The Apostle Peter revealed this in **Acts 2:38** when he was asked what was going on as the Lord's disciples suddenly began to speak in other languages that the foreigners present understood:

"Then Peter said unto them, Repent, and be baptized every one of you in the name of Jesus Christ for the remission of sins, **and ye shall receive the gift of the Holy Ghost.**"

The Spiritual Gifts outlined in **1 Corinthians 12:7-11** are given to us by the Lord Jesus through the Holy Spirit. They are operated in us by the **Holy Spirit** when and how He chooses:

"But the manifestation of the Spirit is given to every man to profit withal. *8* For to one is given by the Spirit **the word of wisdom; to another the word of knowledge by the same Spirit;** *9* **To another faith by the same Spirit; to another the gifts of healing by the same Spirit;**

10 **To another the working of miracles; to another prophecy; to another discerning of spirits; to another divers kinds of tongues; to another the interpretation of tongues:** *11* But all these worketh that one and the selfsame Spirit, dividing to every man severally as he will."

These spiritual **Gifts** can be transferred or imparted from one person to another. This is why the Apostle Paul wanted to visit the believers in Rome so that he can impart to them these **Gifts —Romans 1:10-11**:

"Making request, if by any means now at length I might have a prosperous journey by the will of God to come unto you. *11* **For I long to see you, that I may impart unto you some spiritual gift, to the end ye may be established.**"

The Holy Spirit is God's Seal on all Believers

Some years ago, the Lord showed me in a vision how He used the **Holy Spirit** to write His name **'Jesus'** in His blood on the believers' foreheads. **This is why ungodly people cannot stand a truly Born Again Christian because they carry the blood of Jesus on their foreheads everywhere they go and it changes the spiritual atmosphere.** Evil spirits cannot stand this because it makes them feel threatened.

It is the reason why as a Born Again Christian, you do not have to do anything to make the <u>human carriers of these evil spirits</u> hate you. They will hate you because they do not like **the blood of Jesus** that you bring around them and some of these people are your family members, friends, colleagues, etc. Lack of this knowledge makes **some Born Again Christians unable to understand why they cannot get unbelievers to like them no matter how hard they try or how much they do for them.** Know therefore, that you cannot be accepted by some unbelievers because of **the blood of Jesus** on you. The spirits in them want to run from you and out of the place where you are.

The Bible says that the **Holy Spirit** is God's **Earnest Gift** to us; **the proof that He has redeemed us and that He is coming back to take us to heaven.** It is just like when you want to buy a house and you have to show that you are serious about buying it by putting down **'Earnest Money.'** This earnest money is **a guarantee** that you are willing to go forward with the purchase because it is usually nonrefundable. **The Holy Spirit is also God's <u>Guarantee</u> to us that He has purchased us with the blood of His Son Jesus.**

This is one of the reasons why <u>if you do not know right now</u> that you are born of the Spirit of God in Christ and that you are going to heaven, chances are that you are not going. **In other words, if you are an adult and you have not made the Lord Jesus your Lord, you are not going to find yourself**

in heaven by any other way. Even being 'raptured'(meaning being caught up to be with the Lord) is the <u>work</u> of the **Holy Spirit**. You must know that you belong to the Lord Jesus and that you are filled with the Holy Spirit, sealed with the blood of Jesus before you can think of heaven as your final destination — **Ephesians 1:13-14:**

> "In whom ye also trusted, after that ye heard the word of truth, the gospel of your salvation: in whom also after that ye believed, **ye were sealed with that holy Spirit of promise,** 14 **Which is the earnest of our inheritance until the redemption of the purchased possession,** unto the praise of his glory."

And in **Romans 8:9:**

> "But ye are not in the flesh, but in the Spirit, if so be that the Spirit of God dwell in you. **Now if any man have not the Spirit of Christ, he is none of his.**"

We are God's purchased possession and the 'down payment' that God made on us is the <u>Holy Spirit</u>. This 'down payment' shows that God has truly bought us with the blood of Jesus Christ, that we belong to Him and that He is coming back for us. **This is the reason why no one will wake up and suddenly find themselves in heaven without belonging to the Lord Jesus.** The Lord Jesus is the <u>**only Way**</u> to God (John 14:4).

The Lord Holy Spirit is the Spirit of Grace

The Lord Holy Spirit is the **Grace** of God that enables us to do all that the Lord Jesus commanded us to do. God in His mercy gave us the grace to do all that He wants us to do for Him and to live everyday victoriously because we need Him to do all things. This is why the Lord said in John 15:5, **"Without me you can do nothing."** Unbelievers (those without Jesus as their Lord) live in the <u>**general grace**</u> of God without knowing what God does for them every day. **They do not know that** even being able to wake up and to get out of bed every morning is the result of this Grace but unfortunately, many of them do not want to humble themselves to receive God's Grace of salvation.

Some mock the Christians who try to tell them the '**Good News**' of salvation because they think that they are 'good people' since they have not killed anyone or committed any overt sin. **They refuse to accept that unless they receive God's grace of salvation, they will face the wrath of God and its punishment on Judgment Day.** We see this in **John 3:36**:

> "He that believeth on the Son hath everlasting life: and **he that believeth not the Son shall not see life; but the wrath of God abideth on him.**"

There are some 'Christians' that will also face the wrath of God because they profess Christ with their mouth but live their lives in sin. The Holy Spirit helps us to repent when we sin but those who insist on living in sin and do not change their ways after knowing Christ, are "doing despise" to the Spirit of Grace. There is no more grace for those who abuse the Spirit of Grace by despising Him or His works as we see in **Hebrews 10:29**:

> "Of how much sorer punishment, suppose ye, shall he be thought worthy, who hath trodden underfoot the Son of God, and hath counted the blood of the covenant, wherewith he was sanctified, an unholy thing, **and hath done despite unto the Spirit of grace**?"

Also, to sin against the **Holy Spirit** is serious because He is the channel for our grace. If you cut off the **Spirit of Grace**, there is no more entrance to get grace; it is over!

We see the Grace of the Holy Spirit in **Numbers 11:10-25** when Moses complained that the task given to him by God was too much and that he was not able to bear it by himself alone. In response, God took from the spirit that was on Moses and put it on seventy other people to help him. It proved what the Lord Jesus said that <u>we need Him to accomplish what God gives us to do</u> and to live daily:

> "Then Moses heard the people weep throughout their families, every man in the door of his tent: and the anger of the LORD was kindled greatly; Moses also was displeased. 11 And Moses said unto the LORD, **Wherefore hast thou afflicted thy servant? and wherefore have I not found favour in thy sight, that thou layest the burden of all this people upon me?**
>
> 12 **Have I conceived all this people? have I begotten them, that thou shouldest say unto me, Carry them in thy bosom, <u>as a nursing father beareth the sucking child</u>, unto the land which thou swarest unto their fathers? 13 Whence should I have flesh to give unto all this people? for they weep unto me, saying, Give us flesh, that we may eat. 14 <u>I am not able to bear all this people alone, because it is too heavy for me.</u>**
>
> 15 <u>**And if thou deal thus with me, kill me, I pray thee, out of hand, if I have found favor in thy sight; and let me not see my wretchedness**</u>... 25 And the LORD came down in a cloud, and spake unto him *(Moses)*, **and took of the spirit that was upon him, and gave it unto the Seventy elders: and it came to pass, that, when the spirit rested upon them, they prophesied, and did not cease.**"

As seen above, Moses was getting overburdened by the people that he was leading out of Egypt. Can you imagine just how much Moses was overburdened by the peoples' complains, murmurings and even talks of stoning him? **He was so tired of it all that he told God to kill him right then rather than leave him in the situation he was in with the**

people. In response, God took from **His own Spirit of grace** that was upon Moses and put it on seventy elders so that they can help Moses. These seventy elders began to do what Moses was doing all by himself!

The lesson from Moses' situation is that when you are given an assignment that becomes too heavy for you, <u>ask God to help you</u> by giving you the grace you need. He will give you the grace to accomplish the assignment so that you do not have to struggle and begin to murmur, complain and have a bad attitude.

The Holy Spirit is Our Comforter

We know the Lord Jesus as our Comforter and as a result, we call on His name and ask Him for comfort when we need it. Before He left the earth to return to heaven, He told us in **John 14:15-17** that He will "pray the Father to send us **Another Comforter;**" the **Holy Spirit**:

> "If ye love me, keep my commandments. *16* **And I will pray the Father, and he shall give you <u>another Comforter</u>, that he may abide with you forever;** 17 **Even the Spirit of truth; whom the world cannot receive, because it seeth him not, neither knoweth him**: but ye know him; for <u>he dwelleth with you</u>, and shall be in you…"

The **Holy Spirit** comforts us when we are sick, discouraged, sad or in crisis. At these times, the Holy Spirit comes and He very gently shows us God's love by comforting us with a Word or a song. Although we do not see Him at work, He blows the Father's love upon us and He holds us tenderly when we are down. He ministers God's love to us.

The Holy Spirit is Our Teacher

The **Lord Holy Spirit** is also our teacher as the Lord Jesus informed us in **John 14:26**. It is through the ministry of the

Holy Spirit that we receive answers to the questions we ask the Lord or God the Father and receive instructions or commandments on a daily basis. He teaches us about God the Father, the Lord Jesus and Himself. He can also teach us about anything that we ask Him; even how to pray and what to pray:

> **"But the Comforter, which is the Holy Ghost,** whom the Father will send in my name, **he shall teach you all things, and bring all things to your remembrance,** whatsoever I have said unto you."

I actually came to understand what it means to have the **Holy Spirit** as our teacher in my personal life as I walk with the Lord. **One day, during one of God the Father's visitations, He gave me what I thought at the time to be an 'impossible assignment' because it involved my knowing everything in heaven and the whole world!** I stood before Him flabbergasted by His request and He just smiled in response to my look of bewilderment. As for me, I asked myself, how in the world was I going to know all of the things that God the Father wanted me to know about heaven and this whole world?

For days, months and years, I wondered why God will give me this 'impossible assignment' and I had no answers. One day, I read the scripture above that says that the Holy Spirit **"will teach you all things." I jumped up and I did a dance because the Holy Spirit was the solution to my assignment.** I did not personally have to "know all things" because He does! Oh, I was glad to learn this. All I had to do is rely on the Holy Spirit and He will teach me everything I need to know.

If there is something you do not know, all you have to do is ask the Lord Holy Spirit and He will tell you. **I now use the above scripture every day before I read my Bible because I want understanding of the Word.** I pray, *"Lord, teach me Your Word; help me to know what I am reading. Open my eyes to* *see revelations and mysteries about You and Your Kingdom. Help me to retain what I read, to do the Word and to teach it to others."* Otherwise, you might be trying to study the Word and the devil can send a little evil wind that will put you to sleep while you are holding your Bible.

The Lord Holy Spirit is the Nurturing Side of God

The **Lord Holy Spirit** is soft, caring, nurturing, and gentle. He is the Spirit that nurtures. For example, after surgery, I was in the bed and in pain so I cried out to God and right before dozing off, I saw the Holy Spirt above me. He was blowing a very gentle wind on me and I realized that it was His wind that was putting me to sleep. I looked at Him and I thanked Him for coming to take care of me. It was such a blessing to know that He had come to care and comfort me from the pain. Truly, He is the tender side of God and we see this in **Isaiah 66:13**:

"As one **whom his mother comforteth, so will I comfort you**; and ye shall be comforted in Jerusalem."

This nurturing grace is given by God to every mother but some mothers choose not to receive it. It enables them to gently nurture and comfort their babies. As you have noticed by now, God teaches me with the things that happen to me. <u>In one of these experiences, God allowed me to see His comforting and nurturing anointing on mothers</u>. In this experience, I had been witnessing to one of my neighbors that was a Muslim woman and I was not getting anywhere with her. While I was thinking about it, the Lord said to me, "What she needs is someone to help her watch her baby while she studies."

Before this time, I did not know that she was working on her Desertion so, I approached her about babysitting her son so she can study. She very happily accepted my request but as it turned out, she had one of those babies that do not like anyone to hold them except their mothers. When I picked this baby up, he began to scream at the top of his lungs as though someone was hurting him. I tried to play with him, tried his toys but he would not let up. **To my amazement, when his mother got up to come over to him, <u>I watched as an anointing lifted from her breasts, it made a beeline for the baby and rested on him</u>. Even before she got to the baby, he stopped crying.**

I was shocked at what I had just witnessed and I said to the Lord, "She is not a believer" and **the Lord told me that I had just seen the nurturing and comforting anointing that is upon all mothers.** <u>When a baby cries and the mother makes a move towards the baby, this anointing reaches the baby before the mother touches the baby</u>. This is why when babies are breast feeding, they are being nurtured and comforted. **As they feed, play and express joy while on their mothers' breasts; they are testifying of God's goodness.**

There was a time in my life that I thought that God had singled me out for life's adversities and so, I would cry a lot. One day after my salvation, I was sitting on the ground in my apartment crying and the Lord Jesus just walked in. He sat down beside me on the floor and He did not say a word; He laid my head on His shoulder. He began to rock me back and forth as a mother would her child to let the child know that it would be alright.

At other times, I would see Him wiping my tears away and after a while, I realized that I was going through a 'process' that He had for me; I was not going to be able to cry or pray it away. I decided to let Him 'process me' so that I can overcome and He could then use me to help others. **It is not easy dealing with the problems of life but knowing that the Lord Jesus is going through it with us helps.** He is our Shepherd who nurtures, feeds us and wants to be with us no matter what we are going through — **Isaiah 40:11**:

"He shall feed his flock like a shepherd: he shall gather the lambs with his arm, and <u>carry them</u> in his bosom, and **shall gently lead those that are with young**."

Carrying the young is what mothers do when they have a baby that cannot walk. For those that can walk, they take them by the hand and lead them as they walk together. The Lord promised us that even when a mother decides to be heartless towards her children, He the Lord will not forget to show us compassion and love — **Isaiah 49:15-16**:

"**Can a woman forget her sucking child, that she should not have compassion on the son of her womb? yea, they may forget, yet will I not forget thee.** 16 **Behold, I have graven thee upon the palms of my hands**; thy walls are continually before me."

The Lord Holy Spirit is the Warrior Side of God

Our God is a **Warrior** and He is known in scripture as the **Man of War**, the **Lord of Hosts** and **He wars by His Spirit** — Exodus 15:3:

"**The LORD is a man of war**: the LORD is his name."

And in **2 Samuel 22:16** that when God arises to battle, even creation is not spared:

"And the channels of the sea appeared, the foundations of the world were discovered, at the rebuking of the LORD, **at the blast of the breath of his nostrils**."

The **Lord Holy Spirit** is the one that leads the way in battle and He is the **Spirit that dwelt in Christ**. It was the Holy Spirit that helped the Lord Jesus to overcome the devil's principalities, powers, hell, death and the grave. He also led the army of Israel in battles and we see Him in **Joshua 5:14-15**:

"And he said, **Nay; but as captain of the host of the LORD am I now come**. And Joshua fell on his face to the earth, and did worship, and said unto him, What saith my lord unto his servant? 15 **And the captain of the LORD'S host said unto Joshua, Loose thy shoe from off thy foot; for the place whereon thou standest is holy.** And Joshua did so."

If you declare war with God, the **Holy Spirit** is the one that will answer you. I saw this firsthand in a vision:

"In this vision, God the Father was my husband and you can tell that I was used to getting whatever I wanted because, He had bought me a convertible Mercedes and I was apparently out shopping. I had filled the car up with all types of shopping bags and I had ran out of money. I must have called Him to send me some more money but He did not and as a result, I was furious as I drove back home to this mansion.

*As soon as I entered the front door, I saw Him standing at the top of the staircase dressed in navy blue trousers, navy blue shoes and a sweater just like a regular husband would dress. I was running up the stairs in anger intending to choke Him for not sending me what I requested. As I was running up the staircase, the **Holy Spirit** acting as the '**Butler**' suddenly appeared and in a booming voice demanded to know who I was by saying, "**Who is this?**" In response, **God the Father** said, "She is my wife." and the **Holy Spirit** let me pass.*

You would think that my encounter with the Holy Spirit would have quelled my anger but I was determined as I rushed up to God the Father who was still standing at the top of the stairs to choke Him but before my hands could reach His neck, He did a 'Karate side turn' and I missed Him altogether! Stepping further aside to reveal the upper room behind Him, He said to me, "Tada" as He showed me the tables that He has been preparing for me.

*All the while I thought He was late in answering me, He was busy filling the tables for me. In this upper room were tables from wall to wall and on them was everything I can ever desire and more. He went above and beyond to surpass my desires with His provisions for me on these tables. He then turned and looked at me fiercely as He said, "**Until you become the wife that I can come home to, I will not let you...**"*

After this vision, I knew that I had to adjust my attitude and stop fighting with God. I cried out to Him to make me a good wife for Him. God does not want us to fight with Him but for us to let Him fight for us. There are also times that the Lord comes to fight for you. He once showed up as the **Son of David** and was dressed as a Shepherd as He went after the evil forces that had risen against me. I watched as He began to fling them out one by one and afterwards, He stood at a stance with both His hands on His hips as He asked me, "**Who else is bothering you? Anybody else you want me to take care of?**"

The Lord Jesus wars with the Power of the Holy Spirit. He was the power upon the Lord on the day that He went into the Temple in Jerusalem and drove out those who bought and sold as well as the money changers. **Also, He was the one who took the stone that young David threw and sank into the forehead of Goliath the giant.** We have to know the Lord Holy Spirit as **the warrior side of God** because He is the one who **goes to war on behalf of the believers**.

Summary of the Characteristics of the Holy Spirit
- He can be **breath of life** (in Adam and all human beings)
- He is **wind**
- He is **fire**
- He can be **water**
- He is **God's Gift to us**
- He is the **Holy oil** — the Anointing
- He is the **Spirit of prophecy** (Revelation 19:10)

- He is the **eye of God**
- He the **Spirit of Truth**
- He uses **God's Word to produce what God says**
- He is **our teacher**
- He **reproves the world of sin** — He is **the finger** of God (John 16:7-15)
- He **reveals the things of God to us** (1 Corinthians 2:9)
- He **helps us to pray God's will** (Romans 8:26)
- He **helps us to avoid the work of the flesh** (John 11:5)
- He **can be <u>wounded</u>** because He is very gentle and humble
- He is the **Spirit of Grace** (Matthew 12:31-32)

Chapter 3
Understanding the Spirit of Knowledge

Definition of Knowledge
Knowledge is defined as facts, information and skills acquired by a person through experience or education. It is a person's awareness or familiarity gained by experience of a fact or a situation. This chapter will be about the biblical knowledge that we gain by studying the Word of God and spending time with Him to get intimately acquainted with Him.

Knowledge through Studying the Word of God
We study the Word of God to gain **knowledge of God, His character** and **His ways**. The Bible has all <u>the general information</u> that God wants us to know about Him. As we spend time with Him in prayer and in studying His Word, He gives us <u>**more personal**</u> understanding or knowledge about Himself. As a result, we get to know Him better each time we spend time with Him.

Knowledge is the first thing that God wants us to have. Not just any knowledge but the **true knowledge** of Him. Knowing Him this way is important to God as I found out in my personal life. I had prayed many prayers and some of them God answered but the ones that I deemed most important, went unanswered. As a result, I began to demand God's response as to why my prayer petitions were not answered by Him. In response, He showed a vision:

"In this vision, <u>God the Father dressed like a college professor in a white coat</u>, took me to His classroom in heaven and His classroom has a board on the wall that He writes on. We were standing side by side in front of the board and He said to me, **"You have prayed many prayers."** *He picked up a chalk, walked over to the board and He allowed me to see what was on the board.* **Written in His handwriting were all the**

prayers that I have ever prayed and according to Him, all the prayers that I will ever pray in my life.

I saw that not one of my prayers that I have ever prayed had fallen to the ground! **He gave me time to look them over and I noticed that He had listed all the prayers in <u>His order of priority</u>.** *The first item on the list was,* **knowledge** *followed by* **wisdom, understanding** *and so on...* **He went to the left side of the board; to the beginning of the list of prayers and <u>He checked off Knowledge</u> with His chalk.** *He turned to me and said,* **"What you need is <u>knowledge</u> because you are yet too ignorant for all these other things you have asked for."**

As a result of the vision, I decided to read and reread the Bible continually so that I can gain knowledge. I wanted to know Him and gain more personal knowledge about Him. I knew that by spending time with Him in His Word, I can know Him better and walk more effectively with Him. **From God's perspective, we get knowledge from reading the Bible but He does not want us to stop there because He wants us to gain personal knowledge about what we read in His Word.** It is the Lord Holy Spirit that helps us to do this.

What I learned from my encounter and thus far, is that if you really want to walk with God but you do not have the 'basic building block' which is **His Word**, you will not be able to. You need a solid foundation which the Lord Holy Spirit gives as you thirst for **knowledge** of God and His Word.

The Knowledge that God Desires from Us

The type of knowledge that God wants from us is not head knowledge of the Bible. We are to cry out and diligently search for it as it is revealed in **Proverbs 2:3-20**:

"Yea, **if thou <u>criest</u> after knowledge, and <u>liftest up thy voice</u> for understanding**; 4 If thou **<u>seekest her as silver</u>, and <u>searchest for her as for hid treasures</u>**; 5

Then shalt thou understand the fear of the LORD, and find the knowledge of God...

8 He keepeth the paths of judgment, and preserveth the way of his saints. 9 **Then shalt thou understand righteousness, and judgment, and equity** (fairness); **yea, every good path.**

10 When wisdom entereth into thine heart, and knowledge is pleasant unto thy soul; 11 Discretion shall preserve thee, understanding shall keep thee: 12 To deliver thee from the way of the evil man, from the man that speaketh froward things; 13 Who leave the paths of uprightness, to walk in the ways of darkness...

16 **To deliver thee from the strange woman, even from the stranger which flattereth with her words;** 17 Which forsaketh the guide of her youth, and forgetteth the covenant of her God. 18 For her house inclineth unto death, and her paths unto the dead. 19 None that go unto her return again, neither take they hold of the paths of life. 20 **That thou mayest walk in the way of good men, and keep the paths of the righteous."**

My deeper search for the type of knowledge that God wants began during one of my teaching sessions. **As I was teaching in a certain place, someone busted into tears and asked me why he was not seeing the manifestations of the promises of God in his life?** According to him, he has been waiting for years and nothing has happened and I could tell that he was feeling discouraged in his Christian walk. **I could immediately relate to him because, I was also waiting for the manifestations of many of God's promises to me even after my encounter with Him and He told me that Knowledge was what I needed.** I had read and reread the Bible to gain knowledge but was still waiting. Some of the promises I was waiting on were personally spoken to me face to face by God, in visions, dreams, during prayer and in prophetic words. You probably have also received prophetic words or personal promises from the Lord and you are wondering how long before they come to pass.

That night, I went to the Lord and I told him that the guy has a valid point and that I wanted to know why we all seemed to be waiting for answers from Him. **He reminded me of the vision that He showed me while I was with Him in His classroom and how He had checked off knowledge while telling me that Knowledge was what I needed.** He then informed me that after our encounter, I started reading the Bible more and more because **I thought that He meant for me to read the Bible more**. According to Him, I was viewing receiving knowledge from my own perspective instead His perspective!

This is what God wants to see in us: When we gain the true knowledge of the Word of God, it will change the way we behave. In other words, when we gain true knowledge, we begin to exercise discretion; without which we act foolishly and get ensnared by the devil. **True knowledge teaches us when to keep our mouths shut, when to speak, when to go on and when to stand.** It becomes **our guild** so, take the time to **get the knowledge** of what you are reading in the Bible by letting the Lord Holy Spirit open your eyes as He makes Himself personal to you; **He activates what is written in the Bible to give us a personal knowledge of God.**

This is why knowledge is the 'building block' that the Holy Spirit will use to give you the understanding that demonstrates wisdom in your actions. We all need this because if we believe wrong, we will act wrong no matter how much of the Bible we have read. On the other hand, if we believe right, we will act right and only the Lord Holy Spirit will help us "rightly divide the Word of God." **Therefore, ask**

Him for understanding of what you are reading in the Bible. For example, some minsters on TV use the Word of God in ways that He did not intend for it to be used.

You can see some of them preach about money contrary to the Spirit or intentions of the Word of God for only 15 minutes and then take 45 minutes to collect money. **They tell people to tithe on money they have not yet received or sow a 'seed faith' for money they are hoping to get in the future.** Watching them with a discerning spirit, it is obvious what they are out to do. This is one of the reasons why you need wisdom to keep you and to help you discern what is right and what is wrong by having **proper knowledge** of the Word of God.

God Tests Our Knowledge

God made me to understand that yes, reading the Bible by the help of the Holy Spirit will give us **general knowledge** about Him but **He tests us to see if we have really acquired true knowledge of who He really is**. I have found out that God really **tests our knowledge** through the wisdom we display. **If you are reading the Bible everyday but it does not show in your belief and your behavior, all you are showing is that you are just gathering information from the Bible.** The Word of God in the Bible is meant to be an image in a mirror for us and as we look at the image, become the image reflected by the Word:

> **"But we all, with open face beholding as in a glass the glory of the Lord, are changed into the same image** from glory to glory, **even as by the Spirit of the Lord"** (2 Corinthians 3:18).

Therefore, if you are not being changed by the Word of God that you read in the Bible, lack of God's wisdom will be what is displayed by your actions. In other words, you are not profiting from what the Word is supposed to do for you by the power of the Holy Spirit. Therefore, you should read the Bible to gain wisdom and **true knowledge** so that you can display God's wisdom by your actions.

Chapter 4
Understanding the Spirit of Wisdom

Definition of Wisdom

Wisdom is defined as having experience, knowledge, **good judgement** and the quality of being wise; **the soundness of an action or decision** with regard to the application of experience. For example, the Lord sometimes spoke in parables because the **Word of God is a mystery** and it takes the Holy Spirit to get the understanding. **It is not given to anyone who is not fully committed to God to have the wisdom of the mysteries of the Kingdom of God.**

It is not just unbelievers that have problems knowing the true meaning of the Words the Lord spoke but some believers also. We have to get with the Holy Spirit so that He can teach us scriptures. What the Lord said in **Matthew 13:13-15** is also applicable to those who do not get with the Holy Spirit for His teaching:

> "**Therefore speak I to them in parables: because <u>they seeing see not</u>; and <u>hearing they hear</u> not, neither do they understand**. *14* And in them is fulfilled the prophecy of Esaias, which saith, **By hearing ye shall hear, and shall not understand; and seeing ye shall see, and shall not perceive:**
>
> *15* For this people's heart is waxed gross, and their ears are dull of hearing, and their eyes they have closed; lest at any time they should see with their eyes, and hear with their ears, and should understand with their heart, and should be converted, and I should heal them."

This is one of the reasons that we see some preachers misinterpreting the Word of God because they only know the **letter of the Word** and not the **spirit of the Word**. In other words, although they are preaching the Word of God, they lack the **true wisdom** of it. Of course, you have those who are misusing it for their own gain. They are walking in the wisdom of the world.

God calls the wisdom of the world foolishness. For example, the world calls an atheist, one of the "greatest scientists" whoever lived and he died in his belief that God does not exist **but God saw him as one of the greatest fools who ever lived.** What a difference! Who the world sees as so smart, God sees as one of the most foolish men to ever live. In **Psalm 53:1-4**, we see that this is the general state of the world today and many so called scientists and Astro Physicists promote this ungodly belief. While the world lauds them as great, the Word of God calls them fools:

> **"The fool hath said in his heart, There is no God.** Corrupt are they, and have done abominable iniquity: there is none that doeth good. 2 **God looked down from heaven upon the children of men, to see if there were any that did understand, that did seek God.** 3 Every one of them is gone back: they are altogether become filthy; there is none that doeth good, no, not one. 4 **Have the workers of iniquity no knowledge?..."**

Apparently not, because as we have seen that true knowledge and wisdom only come from the Lord Holy Spirit. **This is why some Christians have even abandoned their faith in Christ because they never really got to know the Lord Jesus and some of them have now joined the bandwagons of fools who claim that God does not exist.** Meanwhile, the devil blinds them to the fact that they do not have the knowledge of all of creation or the entire universe to accurately conclude that God does not exist.

God purposely hid His wisdom from those who want nothing to do with Him. Since ancient times, people have tried to understand this world without the wisdom of God and they have all failed. In **Job 28:21**, we see that, "**Wisdom is hid from all living.**" Also, according to **1 Corinthians 2:6-8**, **wisdom is also hidden** from the devil and his demons:

> "Howbeit we speak wisdom among them that are perfect: **yet not the wisdom of this world, nor of the princes of this world, that come to nought:** 7 **But we speak the wisdom of God in a mystery, even the hidden wisdom, which God ordained before the world unto our glory:** 8 **Which <u>none of the princes of this world knew</u>: for <u>had they known it, they would not have crucified the Lord of glory</u>.**"

As Christians, we must stay away from the wisdom of this world. It is straight from the pit of hell because as the Bible says of the world in **Romans 1:22**, "**Professing themselves to be wise, they became fools.**"

The Importance of Wisdom

Wisdom is so important that **Proverbs 3:13-26** tell us that it is more precious than silver, gold or diamonds. Nothing can compare to the value of the **Wisdom** that God gives us:

> "**Happy is the man that <u>findeth wisdom</u>, and the man that getteth understanding.** 14 **For the merchandise of it is <u>better than the merchandise of silver</u>, and the gain thereof than fine gold.** 15 <u>She is more precious than rubies: and all the things thou canst desire are not to be compared unto her</u>. 16 Length of days is in her right hand; and in her left hand riches and honour.
>
> 17 **Her ways are ways of pleasantness, and all her paths are peace.** 18 She is a tree of life to them that lay hold upon her: and happy is every one that retaineth her. 19 **The LORD by wisdom hath founded the earth;** by understanding hath he established the heavens. 20 By his knowledge the depths are broken up, and the clouds drop down

the dew. 21 My son, let not them depart from thine eyes: keep sound wisdom and discretion:

22 So shall they be life unto thy soul, and grace to thy neck. 23 Then shalt thou walk in thy way safely, and thy foot shall not stumble. 24 When thou liest down, thou shalt not be afraid: yea, thou shalt lie down, and thy sleep shall be sweet. 25 Be not afraid of sudden fear, neither of the desolation of the wicked, when it cometh. 26 For the LORD shall be thy confidence, and shall keep thy foot from being taken."

It is not enough to gain wisdom one time but you must retain wisdom throughout your lifetime. You cannot have just head knowledge of the Word because it will make you become puffed up and religious. As you read the Word of God and you let the Holy Spirit help you process it, you will see that the Word of God will change you and make you **Christ-like** and you will display sound godly **wisdom**.

Chapter 5
Knowing the Spirit of Understanding

Definition of Understanding:

Understanding means having **insight** or **good judgement**; the ability to understand something and comprehend it. It also means to be sympathetically aware of other people's feelings. **If you tell yourself that you are getting understanding, God will have to put you to the test to see if you are really getting understanding or just accumulating words from the Bible.**

As we have seen thus far, you must first get **understanding** so that wisdom and knowledge can be reflected in your actions. **Until you are reflecting them in your judgements, God says that you have no <u>understanding of what you are reading in His Word</u>**. Therefore, you must make sure that you are getting **understanding**. This is emphasized in **Proverbs 4:7**:

> "Wisdom is the principal thing; therefore get wisdom: **and with all thy getting get <u>understanding</u>.**"

Wisdom is good but without **understanding**, it will not do much good in your life. This is why we are told to get understanding along with wisdom. The question asked in **Job 28:12-27** is: Where do we get wisdom and **understanding**? The Holy Spirit is the answer to this question:

> **"But where shall wisdom be found? and where is the place of understanding? 13 <u>Man</u>** knoweth not the **<u>price</u>** thereof; neither is it found in the land of the living. 14 **<u>The depth</u>** (under the earth) saith, It is not in me: and **<u>the sea</u>** saith, It is not with me. 15 **<u>It cannot be gotten for gold</u>, neither shall silver be weighed for the price thereof. 16 It cannot be valued with the gold of Ophir, with the precious onyx, or the sapphire.**
>
> 17 The **<u>gold and the crystal cannot equal it</u>: and <u>the exchange of it shall not be for jewels of fine gold</u>.** 18 No mention shall be made of coral, or of pearls: **for**

the price of wisdom is above rubies. *19* The topaz of Ethiopia shall not equal it, neither shall it be valued with pure gold. *20* **Whence then cometh wisdom? and where is the place of understanding?**

21 **Seeing it is <u>hid from the eyes of all living</u>, and kept <u>close from the fowls of the air</u>. *22* Destruction and death** say, We have heard the fame thereof with our ears. *23* **God <u>understandeth the way thereof, and he knoweth the place thereof</u>**. *24* For he looketh to the ends of the earth, and seeth under the whole heaven; *25* To make the weight for the winds; and he weigheth the waters by measure. *26* When he made a decree for the rain, and a way for the lightning of the thunder: *27* **Then did he see it, and declare it**; he prepared it, yea, and searched it out."

The scripture above shows how precious and how important God views **Wisdom** and **understanding**. To Him, they are worth more than all the rubies of more value than all the gold in the world. If you search for them by yourself, you are not going to find them and you will just end up being able to quote the Bible very well. **This is why the Bible says, "<u>The lettter killeth</u>, it is the spirit that giveth life."** It is easy for people to quote the Bible and teach the Bible but if they are not living according to the Word, they do not really have the **understanding** that God wants. **To Him, all <u>they have is information</u>**. Our goal therefore, is to get **understanding** because understanding and wisdom show that we have the **true Knowledge of God.** That is why **Proverbs 2:1-20** tells us:

"My son, if thou wilt receive my words, and hide my commandments with thee; *2* So that thou incline thine ear unto <u>wisdom</u>, and apply thine heart to **understanding;** *3* Yea, if thou **criest after <u>knowledge</u>, and liftest up thy voice for<u> understanding</u>;** *4* If thou **seekest her as silver, and searchest for her as for hid treasures;** *5* <u>Then shalt thou understand the fear of the Lord, and find the knowledge of God.</u>

6 For the Lord giveth wisdom: out of his mouth cometh knowledge and understanding. *7* He layeth up sound wisdom for the righteous: he is a buckler to them that walk uprightly. *8* He keepeth the paths of judgment, and preserveth the way of his saints. **9 Then shalt thou understand righteousness, and judgment, and equity; yea, every good path. 10 When wisdom entereth into thine heart, and knowledge is pleasant unto thy soul;**

11 Discretion shall preserve thee, **understanding shall keep thee:** *12* To deliver thee from the way of the evil man, from the man that speaketh froward things; *13* Who leave the paths of uprightness, to walk in the ways of darkness; *14* Who rejoice to do evil, and delight in the frowardness of the wicked...*20* That thou mayest walk in the way of good men, and keep the paths of the righteous."

Until you get **wisdom** and **understanding,** you cannot achieve the **goal of the true Knowledge of God.** When **wisdom** and understanding are **reflected** in your **actions** and in your **judgements**, then you shall understand righteousness, judgement, equity *(not preferring one person over another)* and every good path. As you see thus far, getting **understanding** is critical to having **true knowledge.** The Bible tells us that this is why the entire book of Proverbs was written as shown in Proverbs 1:1-28:

"The proverbs of Solomon the son of David, king of Israel; *2* To know wisdom and instruction; to perceive the words of understanding; *3* To receive the instruction of wisdom, justice, and judgment, and equity; *4* To give subtilty to the simple, to the young man knowledge and discretion. *5* A wise man will hear, and will increase learning; and a man of understanding shall attain unto wise counsels: *6* To understand a proverb, and the interpretation; the words of the wise, and their dark sayings.

7 The fear of the LORD is the beginning of knowledge: but fools despise wisdom and instruction. 8 My son, hear the instruction of thy father, and forsake not the law of thy mother: 9 For they shall be an ornament of grace unto thy head, and chains about thy neck... 22 How long, ye simple ones, will ye love simplicity? and the scorners delight in their scorning, and fools hate knowledge? 23 Turn you at my reproof: behold, I will pour out my spirit unto you, I will make known my words unto you.

24 Because I have called, and ye refused; I have stretched out my hand, and no man regarded; 25 But ye have set at nought all my counsel, and would none of my reproof: 26 I also will laugh at your calamity; I will mock when your fear cometh; 27 When your fear cometh as desolation, and your destruction cometh as a whirlwind; when distress and anguish cometh upon you. 28 Then shall they call upon me, but I will not answer; they shall seek me early, but they shall not find me."

The true knowledge and **understanding** of God will produce a good night sleep. **Also, if you are praying for riches and honor to be manifested in your life and they are not, then you are not walking in understanding according to Proverbs 3:16**. The reason is because **length of days** is in the right hand of **wisdom** and in her left hand are **riches and honor**. You cannot have them when you do not display the understanding of God in your actions.

Even when you want to build anything worthwhile in life, you need **wisdom** and **understanding**. It is why we read the following instructions in **Proverbs 4:1-13**:

"Hear, ye children, the instruction of a father, and attend to know understanding. 2 For I give you good doctrine, forsake ye not my law. 3 For I was my father's son, tender and only beloved in the sight of my mother. 4 He taught me also, and said unto me, Let thine heart retain my words: keep my commandments, and live. 5 **Get wisdom, get understanding**… 8 Exalt her, and she shall promote thee: she shall bring thee to honour, when thou dost embrace her.

9 **She shall give to thine head an ornament of grace:** <u>a crown of glory shall she deliver to thee</u>. 10 Hear, O my son, and receive my sayings; and the years of thy life shall be many. 11 I have taught thee in the way of wisdom; I have led thee in right paths. 12 **When thou goest, thy steps shall not be straitened; and when thou runnest, thou shalt not stumble.** 13 Take fast hold of instruction; let her not go: **keep her; for she is thy life."**

As we have learned, if you do not have godly judgement and your actions do not line up with God's Word, then you do not know Him. **Wisdom and understanding will bring you to a place of a solid foundation in God.**

The Holy Spirit Gives Understanding of Scriptures

We are told in **Proverbs 24:3** that, **"Through wisdom a house is built and by understanding it is established."** A lot of people do not take the meaning of this Proverb to heart and seek God's understanding as they read the Bible. **As a result, they read and reread the Bible to their own confusion.**

The reason that they cannot **understand** the Bible is because, they do not have the right spirit; **the Holy Spirit**. It is the **Holy Spirit** that gives us **understanding** of scriptures. **The result of their not having the Holy Spirit is that they challenge the things that are written in the Bible.** Due to this type of stubborn mindset, the **Holy Spirit** is not going to give them <u>understanding</u> because they have not subjected themselves to the Lordship of Jesus Christ.

These people do not realize that it is <u>important</u> to make Jesus the Lord of their lives and they walk away with the

conclusion that the Bible is just an ordinary book. On the other hand, those who are Spirit-filled interact with God as they read or study the Bible. **On several occasions, the Bible came alive to me as I was reading it.** As a baby Christian, God literally spoke to me through His written Word in the Bible and I closed the Bible because I said, "**This book talks.**" At another time, I was reading the verse in **Proverbs 11:30** that says:

"...And **he that winneth souls is <u>wise</u>.**"

I watched my Bible as the "**W**" in wise <u>lifted off the page and began to take the shape of a human face</u>. I continued to watch as it became a 'life size' God the Father sprawled out across my Bible and smiling! He said to me, "**I told you that I and my Word are One**!" Only God can do this because a 'life size' person cannot fit on the page of a Bible! Yes, I know firsthand that the Bible contains the **Living Word of God** that comes alive to those who are Spirit-filled and are reading it in faith.

Lack of Understanding Makes Us Accuse God Foolishly

The Lord showed me that when I bicker, fight and charge Him foolishly; which I did for many years, I show my **lack of understanding.** I did this until He said to me, "**Until you know me as the God that cannot be blamed, we cannot walk together.**" I say these things to you now because according to Him, **we are entering a time when people will <u>not want</u> the true knowledge of God in their lives. Therefore, if you are someone who finds reasons to <u>judge God</u> or who finds a way to bicker with God, know that you are delaying your blessings by doing this.**

The Word of God in **Isaiah 45:9** said this about those who fight with God:

"**Woe unto him that striveth with his Maker**! Let the potsherd strive with the potsherds of the earth. Shall the clay say to him that fashioneth it, What makest thou? or thy work, He hath no hands?"

If you want to test yourself about whether or not you are growing in the true knowledge and understanding of God, ask yourself this: **Have you been judging God for something that you believe that He has not done or failed to do for you?** If the answer is yes, **then you lack true knowledge and understanding of God.** The key is in **Genesis 1:31** which says that <u>God saw that everything that He made was very good</u>. Therefore, we must all know that **God, His thoughts, His ways** and **His actions** are perfect; He has no blame and cannot be blamed for anything:

> "**And God saw everything that he had made, and, behold, <u>it was very good</u>.**"

This is why those who think that God made a mistake by putting them in the 'wrong body' are very wrong in their belief. God did not make Adam and Steve; He made Adam and Eve. **He made male and female and He is the author of what makes a man and what makes a woman.** He is not the author of confusion so that those who are confused about their genders bear the blame and the society around them. This is why we must all know that God has no faults and He cannot be blamed for anything going wrong in our lives. If there is a problem, you better believe that it is not coming from God's side.

Anyone who does not obey God has **no understanding** of God and His ways. Anyone who walks according to their own will (iniquity), does not know God. Those who judge God for the <u>disappointments</u> in their lives or for **not being there** for them while displaying this **lack of understanding** of God, do not know God. **Wisdom, knowledge and understanding are to help us know that this whole world and our entire lives are about God.** It is all about Him and He owns everything. All souls belong to Him and He is the ultimate goal that we should seek to have in our lives. Knowing this will help us to walk according to His rules and not seek to circumvent them by disobedience.

This is the problem with the world today because many people think that they know so much and do not need to be told about God or anything else. **It is now all about freedom to exercise their rights** and many of them are not interested in the right way or being morally upright. **The love of money and pursuit of personal freedom is what is driving the world today and they do not want anyone telling them what God says.** As a result, evil is being called good and good is being called evil. **Any Christian who does not embrace their ungodly ways is called intolerant or homophobic.**

There are some Christians who support the things that the world does and that God said are abominations. Other Christians help promote these ungodly causes or lend them their support when they find out that their child or someone close to them is involved in an ungodly lifestyle. They shift from being on God's side and begin to support abominable ways; this is a shame. They prove what the Bible said in **1 Corinthians 15:33** that, "Evil communications corrupt good manners."

If you cannot come to a place where you fear God enough to tell your child or close relative the truth about their ungodly lifestyle, then when God sends you and the person you supported to hell, you will only have yourself to blame. The Lord Jesus told us this in **Matthew 10:37**:

> "He that loveth father or mother more than me is not worthy of me: **and he that loveth son or daughter more than me is not worthy of me.**"

All Christians Claim to Love God
Most people and every professing Christian claim to love God even when they are living their lives contrary to His

Word. This is why the Lord Jesus gave us a litmus test to show those who truly love Him. We read this in **John 14:23-24**:

> "Jesus answered and said unto him, **If a man love me, he will keep my words:** and my Father will love him, and we will come unto him, and make our abode with him. 24 **He that <u>loveth me not</u> keepeth not my sayings:** and the word which ye hear is not mine, but the Father's which sent me."

As we can clearly see from the Lord's own lips, those who <u>obey His commandments</u> are those who love Him. **You can go to church and cry every time the pastor shows up and is preaching but if you do not obey the Word of God that comes to you, you do not love the Lord.** In other words, if you do not live according to His Word, you do not love Him. This is why we cannot say that we love Him and support the things that He hates.

Some people lie on the ground with tears and carry on and on about their love for God but when the Word of God says, "Go here," they are too busy to obey. From the Lord's perspective, they do not love Him or His Father. Therefore, we all need to really go back and examine how we have been approaching the **true knowledge** of God through the demonstration of our **wisdom** and **understanding** by <u>our obedience</u>.

Chapter 6
Understanding the Spirit of Counsel

Definition of Counsel

Counsel is defined as an **advice**; especially as a result of consultation. It also means a legal practitioner such as a lawyer, an attorney or a counselor and it is a synonym for **guidance, direction, instruction** or **information**. We saw in **Isaiah 11:1-2** that, one of the **Seven Spirits of God** that will rest on the Messiah is the **Spirit of Counsel**. He needed it to be <u>effective in His duty as **an unbiased Judge**</u>:

> "And there shall come forth a rod out of the stem of Jesse, and a Branch shall grow out of his roots: 2 <u>And the spirit of the LORD shall rest upon him, the spirit of wisdom and understanding, **the spirit of Counsel** and might, the spirit of knowledge and of the fear of the LORD.</u>"

As a result, the Lord Jesus is our **Counselor** and our **Advocate** in heaven before His Father. Here on earth, He gives us **counsel** when we ask Him for it. We all need **God's counsel** in everything that we do because we are told in **Proverbs 15:22** that:

> "**Without counsel <u>purposes are disappointed</u>:** but in the multitude of **counsellors they are established**."

And also in **Proverbs 11:14** that:

> "**Where no counsel is, the people fall**: but in the multitude of counsellors there is safety."

Therefore, we all need godly **Counsel** in every aspect of our lives and **true counsel** comes from the Word of God. This is why the Bible says in **Psalms 119:105**:

> "**Thy word is a <u>lamp</u> unto my feet, and a <u>light</u> unto my path.**"

The counsel from the Word of God lights our feet and our paths through life. Therefore, ask God for His counsel while you are studying His Word and He will give it to you. The Next thing is to listen for the Holy Spirit's instructions. When He tells you to "**do this and not that**," you must listen to Him because He is giving you **godly Counsel**. As you continue to ask for His counsel, He will guide you in the right paths. **Even when you are a student in High school or college, you need the Holy Spirit to activate His counsel in you to help you understand what you are being taught.**

The Old Testament Way of Seeking God's Counsel

The Lord Jesus ushered in the **Grace of God** so that we can have direct communication with God as our Father. During the time of the Law that was given to Moses and beginning with Aaron as the High Priest, the children of Israel used the **Urim** and **Thummim** to <u>ask</u> **counsel** of the Lord. We see this in **Exodus 28:30**:

> "And thou shalt put in the breastplate of judgment the **Urim** and the **Thummim**; and <u>they shall be upon Aaron's heart, when he goeth in before the LORD...</u>"

The people went to the High Priest to seek **counsel** from the Lord and after they have made their request known to the High Priest, he would put his hand in his breastplate. If he brings out **Urim**, it means the answer from the Lord is **Yes** but if he brings out **Thummim**, the answer is **No**. This was how the children of Israel consulted the Lord for **His counsel** as to whether to go to war or not, and whether to do something or not.

When Moses knew that he would soon die, he asked God to give the children of Israel <u>a man that will seek God's counsel for them</u>. We see him making this request to God in **Numbers 27:15-21**:

"And Moses spake unto the LORD, saying, *16* **Let the LORD, the God of the Spirits of all flesh, set a man over the congregation, *17* Which may go out before them, and which may go in before them, and which may lead them out, and which may bring them in; that the congregation of the LORD be not as sheep which have no shepherd.** *18* And the LORD said unto Moses, Take thee Joshua the son of Nun, a man in whom is the spirit, and lay thine hand upon him;

19 And set him before Eleazar the priest, and before all the congregation; and give him a charge in their sight. *20* And thou shalt put some of thine honour upon him, that all the congregation of the children of Israel may be obedient. *21* **And he shall stand before Eleazar the priest, who shall ask counsel for him after the judgment of Urim before the LORD:** at his word shall they go out, and at his word they shall come in, both he, and all the children of Israel with him, even all the congregation."

From the scripture above, we see how important it was in those days for the children of Israel to have the **Urim** and **Thummim** to get **the Counsel of the Lord.**

Failure to Seek God's Counsel

Under the **leadership of Joshua**, the children of Israel were ensnared by the Gibeonites when **they acted according to their own desire without seeking counsel from the Lord — Joshua 9:3-16**:

"And when the **inhabitants of Gibeon** heard what Joshua had done unto Jericho and to Ai, *4* They did work wilily, and went and made as if they had been ambassadors, and took old sacks upon their asses, and wine bottles, old, and rent, and bound up; *5* And old shoes and clouted upon their feet, and old garments upon them; and all the bread of their provision was dry and mouldy.

6 And they went to Joshua unto the camp at Gilgal, and said unto him, and to the men of Israel, **We be come from a far country: now therefore make ye a league with us.** 7 And the men of Israel said unto the Hivites, Peradventure ye dwell among us; and how shall we make a league with you? 8 And they said unto Joshua, We are thy servants. And Joshua said unto them, Who are ye? and from whence come ye?

9 And they said unto him, From a very far country thy servants are come because of the name of the LORD thy God: for we have heard the fame of him, and all that he did in Egypt, 10 And all that he did to the two kings of the Amorites, that were beyond Jordan, to Sihon king of Heshbon, and to Og king of Bashan, which was at Ashtaroth. 11 Wherefore our elders and all the inhabitants of our country spake to us, saying,

Take victuals with you for the journey, and go to meet them, and say unto them, We are your servants: therefore now make ye a league with us. 12 This our bread we took hot for our provision out of our houses on the day we came forth to go unto you; but now, behold, it is dry, and it is mouldy: 13 And these bottles of wine, which we filled, were new; and, behold, they be rent: and these our garments and our shoes are become old by reason of the very long journey.

14 **And the men took of their victuals, and asked not counsel at the mouth of the LORD.** 15 And Joshua made peace with them, and made a league with them, to let them live: and the princes of the congregation sware unto them. 16 And it came to pass at the end of three days after they had made a league with them, that they heard that they were their neighbours, and that they dwelt among them."

God is so righteous that if you **make a covenant with the devil,** He will **honor it** until you repent, renounce and cancel it by the blood of Jesus. One of the reasons for this is because, one of God's titles is, **'The God of Covenants.'** The result of this is that the **above covenant that the children of Israel made with the Gibeonites under the leadership of Joshua, remained in place until the reign of King David who suffered the consequences of King Saul's violation of it**.

After the death of King Saul and during the reign of King David, God began to punish the children of Israel. **There was a <u>famine in Israel for three years</u> and when King David inquired of the Lord as to the cause, the Lord told him that it was because King Saul violated the covenant that Joshua and children of Israel made with the Gibeonites.** As recorded in **2 Samuel 21:1-6**, <u>to stop the famine, King David had to give to the Gibeonites the 7 heads of King Saul's sons</u>:

"Then **there was a famine in the days of David three years, year after year; and David enquired of the LORD. And the LORD answered, It is for Saul, and for his bloody house, because he slew the Gibeonites.** 2 And the king called the Gibeonites, and said unto them; (now the Gibeonites were not of the children of Israel, but of the remnant of the Amorites; and **the children of Israel had sworn unto them** *(made a covenant of peace with them)*:

and Saul sought to slay them *(Killed them)* **in his zeal to the children of Israel and Judah.**) 3 Wherefore David said unto the Gibeonites, What shall I do for you? and wherewith shall I make the atonement, that ye may bless the inheritance of the LORD? 4 And the Gibeonites said unto him, **We will have no silver nor gold of Saul, nor of his house; neither for us shalt thou kill any man in Israel.** <u>And he said, What ye shall say, that will I do for you</u>.

5 And they answered the king, The man that consumed us, and that devised against us that we should be destroyed from remaining in any of the coasts of

Israel, 6 **Let seven men of his sons be delivered unto us, and we will hang them up unto the LORD in Gibeah of Saul, whom the LORD did choose.** And the king said, **I will give them."**

Where Do You Get this Counsel?

You will find **Counsel** in the place where you find wisdom, knowledge and understanding as declared in **Proverbs 8:12-17:**

"I wisdom dwell with prudence, and find out knowledge of witty inventions. 13 The fear of the LORD is to hate evil: pride, and arrogancy, and the evil way, and the froward mouth, do I hate. 14 **Counsel is mine,** and **sound wisdom: I am understanding; I have strength.** 15 By me kings reign, and princes decree justice. 16 By me princes rule, and nobles, even all the judges of the earth. 17 I love them that love me; and **those that seek me early shall find me."**

Wisdom gives you **counsel** that results in you knowing how to be **prudent** and **discrete**. You will no longer be irrational or rash in your decision making because the **Spirit of Counsel** will help you think things through before acting. It will help you to see evil for what it is so that you can walk in wisdom. You will develop a perfect hatred for evil things and you will become humble and not proud anymore. You will also begin to love the things that God loves and you will not run your mouth anymore. **These are things that you will never be able to find outside of the Lord Jesus Christ because they are in Him.**

If you look at the world today, you will see injustice and corruption in every country. This is why God is very patient in making sure that the 'Chosen Generation' that He gave to His Son is large enough **to rule the world with Christ in righteousness in the next age.** It is the reason why He wants many more people to come into His Kingdom because He wants more sons and daughters that will rule the next world for Him. In other words, God needs enough '**New Creations**' (Born Again Christians) <u>to help administer the vast estate of His Kingdom</u> because in the age to come when He sets up His kingdom, He will have **righteous judges** and **righteous counselors** in every level of human government and affairs.

These 'New Creations' will be people who for example when you go to court, you will not be worried about not getting justice or afraid that there will be a miscarriage of justice on your behalf. This 'Chosen Generation' that God gave to His Son, will occupy every position of authority on earth that is currently being held by corrupt people. This is what God meant in **Genesis 1:26,** when He said, "**Let us make man in our <u>image</u> and after our <u>likeness</u>** (character) **and let man have <u>dominion</u>**" over everything that moves over the earth.

The Nature of Counsel

The nature of counsel is that it can be **wise** or **foolish** and it can **good** or **bad**. Unfortunately, most people in the world today choose the <u>foolish counsel of man</u> over the **wise counsel of God** and as a result, walk in defeat. It is God's will that we live by His **godly counsel** which comes only from living by the Word of God. This is why He said in **Deuteronomy 8:3**:

> "… <u>Man doth not live by bread only</u>, **but by every word that proceedeth out of the mouth of the LORD doth man live.**"

The world does not want to live by God's Word. Therefore, God sees the wicked and their wicked counsels and He takes them in their own craftiness. **Also, God can make a person choose a foolish counsel when He wants to bring His judgment to pass against the person and He can also turn a wise counsel to foolishness.**

A Case of a Ruler Choosing a Foolish Counsel

God made Absalom to choose a **foolish counsel** when he rose up against his father; King David. Ahithophel defected with Absalom and became one of Absalom counselors. Before this, Ahithophel was one of King David's most trusted counselors and many regarded his counsel as straight out of the mouth of God — **2 Samuel 16:23**:

> "And **the counsel of Ahithophel, which he counselled in those days, was as if a man had enquired at the oracle of God:** so was all the counsel of Ahithophel both with David and with Absalom."

According to **2 Samuel 11:3, 23:34, Ahithophel** was the father of **Eliam** and **Eliam** was the father of **Bathsheba** who was married to **Uriah** but became King David's favorite wife. **This genealogy shows us that Ahithophel was Bathsheba's grandfather but he turned against King David because of the long time grudge he had against the King for** defiling his married granddaughter.

His counsel to Absalom revealed that all the time that he was giving counsel to King David, he nursed his resentment **against him for the shame that he caused his family.** As a result, when the opportunity came for him to rise up against King David to show his contempt for him, he did so by encouraging Absalom in his insurrection against his father; King David.

Ahithophel's initial counsel to Absalom which he complied with was **for Absalom to publicly defile his father's concubines on the roof top of the palace** in broad daylight and before all Israel in order to show that he was now the King instead of David. **As you can see from this counsel, it was Ahithophel's revenge against King David for defiling his granddaughter even after King David married her and she was his favorite wife** — 2 Samuel 16:20-22:

> "Then said Absalom to Ahithophel, Give counsel among you what we shall do. 21 **And Ahithophel said unto Absalom, Go in unto thy father's concubines,**

which he hath left to keep the house; and all Israel
shall hear that thou art abhorred of thy father: then
shall the hands of all that are with thee be strong.
22 So they spread Absalom a tent upon the top of
the house; **and Absalom went in unto his father's
concubines in the sight of all Israel.**"

No other **counsel of revenge** could have been as powerful as
Ahithophel **perverting the gift of counsel** that God gave him.
King David knew how powerful the **counsel of Ahithophel**
was so, he prayed that God should turn the **wise counsel** of
Ahithophel to **foolishness —2 Samuel 15:31**:

"And one told David, saying, <u>Ahithophel is among
the conspirators with Absalom</u>. And David said, **O
LORD, I pray thee, turn the counsel of Ahithophel
into foolishness.**"

**To defeat David, Ahithophel's counsel to Absalom was to
pursue King David and his followers while they were still
weak and weary. He also told Absalom to allow him to kill
just the King and bring back all those who fled with him**
so that Absalom can establish himself as the uncontested
ruler **—2 Samuel 17:1-4**:

"Moreover Ahithophel said unto Absalom, **Let me
now choose out twelve thousand men, and I will
arise and pursue after David this night:** 2 **And I will
come upon him while he is weary and weak handed,
and will make him afraid: and all the people that are
with him shall flee; and** <u>I will smite the king only</u>:

3 **And I will bring back all the people unto thee**: the
man whom thou seekest is as if all returned: **so all the
people shall be in peace.** 4 And the saying pleased
Absalom well, and all the elders of Israel."

In answer to King David's prayer, Absalom asked **his young
friends** to give him counsel also whether to pursue after

King David or not. <u>Their counsel was not to pursue</u> and Absalom chose their **foolish counsel** over the **wise counsel** of Ahithophel. He did not think Ahithophel's counsel was wise because according to **2 Samuel 17:14**, God made sure that Ahithophel's counsel was defeated so that Absalom might die:

> "And <u>Absalom and all the men of Israel said, The counsel of Hushai the Archite is better than the counsel of Ahithophel.</u> **For the LORD had appointed to defeat the good counsel of Ahithophel, to the intent that the LORD might bring evil upon Absalom.**"

When Ahithophel saw that his counsel was rejected, he went to his house and killed himself! One of God's titles is, '**He takes the wicked in their own craftiness**' and we see it in this case.

Another Case of a Ruler Choosing a Foolish Counsel

You would think that since King Solomon was so wise that his son would be wise also but that did not turn out to be the case with Rehoboam his son. Before King Solomon died, he was listening to the <u>pagan counsels</u> of many his **seven hundred wives** and it angered God because King Solomon built idol temples for many of them. Therefore, **God commanded the Prophet Ahijah to anoint Jeroboam as King** and this greatly disturbed King Solomon and he sought to kill Jeroboam — **1 Kings 11:28-33**:

> "And the man Jeroboam was a mighty man of valour: <u>and Solomon seeing the young man that he was industrious, he made him ruler over all the charge of the house of Joseph.</u> 29 And it came to pass at that time when Jeroboam went out of Jerusalem, that **the prophet Ahijah the Shilonite found him in the way; and he** *(Jeroboam)* **had clad himself with a new garment;** and they two were alone in the field:
>
> 30 **And Ahijah caught the new garment that was on him, and rent it in twelve pieces:** 31 **And he**

said to Jeroboam, Take thee ten pieces: for thus saith the LORD, the God of Israel, Behold, I will rend the kingdom out of the hand of Solomon, and <u>will give ten tribes to thee:</u> 32 (But he shall have one tribe for my servant David's sake, and for Jerusalem's sake, the city which I have chosen out of all the tribes of Israel:)

33 Because that they have forsaken me, and have worshipped Ashtoreth the goddess of the Zidonians, Chemosh the god of the Moabites, and Milcom the god of the children of Ammon, **and have not walked in my ways, to do that which is right in mine eyes, and to keep my statutes and my judgments, as did David his father."**

To fulfill this judgement against King Solomon, God stirred up Jeroboam to come back after King Solomon's death because Jeroboam had fled into exile from King Solomon. **Therefore, Jeroboam was the leader of the multitudes that came to the newly appointed King Rehoboam demanding better conditions under him.** King Rehoboam told them to go and come back in three days and he will give them his answer **—1 Kings 12:3-5**:

"...And Jeroboam and all the congregation of Israel came, and spake unto Rehoboam, saying, 4 **Thy father made our yoke grievous: now therefore make thou the grievous service of thy father, and his heavy yoke which he put upon us, lighter, and we will serve thee.** 5 And he said unto them, Depart yet for three days, then come again to me. And the people departed..."

Just like Absalom, **Rehoboam the son of King Solomon** also chose the **foolish counsel** of his young advisers over the **wise counsel** of the older men. This resulted in his **loss of 10 tribes of Israel** because they rebelled against him and formed their own kingdom with **Jeroboam** as their leader **—1 Kings 12:12-16**:

"So Jeroboam and all the people came to Rehoboam the third day, as the king had appointed, saying, Come to me again the third day. 13 **And the king answered the people roughly, and <u>forsook the old men's counsel that they gave him;</u> 14 And spake to them <u>after the counsel of the young men</u>, saying, My father made your yoke heavy, and I will add to your yoke: my father also chastised you with whips, but I will chastise you with scorpions.**

15 <u>Wherefore the king hearkened not unto the people; for the cause was from the LORD, that he might perform his saying, which the LORD spake by Ahijah the Shilonite unto Jeroboam the son of Nebat.</u> 16 So when all Israel saw that the king hearkened not unto them, the people answered the. king, saying, <u>What</u> portion have we in David? neither have we inheritance in the son of Jesse: **to your tents, O Israel**: **now see to thine own house, David.** So Israel departed unto their tents."

As you can see, King Rehoboam lacked diplomacy and did not <u>choose good</u> or <u>godly counsel</u> in speaking to the people but chose the very foolish counsel of his peers. As a result, only **the tribe of Benjamin** remained with the tribe of Judah. King **Rehoboam's kingdom greatly diminished from twelve to two as a result of the foolish counsel that he chose!**

Again, the Lord can make someone choose a foolish counsel over a wise counsel when He sees that the person is evil or is about to bring His judgement to pass against the person. The book of Proverbs talks a lot about <u>the fool who rejects wise counsel because godly counsel is too high for a fool</u> — **Proverbs 24:7:**

"**Wisdom is too high for a fool**..."

Chapter 7
Understanding the Spirit of Might

As I showed you from the scripture in **Isaiah 11:1-2**, one of the **Seven Spirits of God** that was upon the Lord Jesus was the **Spirit of Might:**

> "And there shall come forth a rod out of the stem of Jesse, and a Branch shall grow out of his roots: 2 And the spirit of the LORD shall rest upon him, the spirit of wisdom and understanding, the spirit of counsel and **Might**, the spirit of knowledge and of the fear the LORD..."

Definition of Might

Might is defined as a **great power or force** such as a nation or army that is superior in power or strength. It also means physical strength such as the capacity or ability to do or accomplish something. For example, a person can push something with all his power and might which is really human effort but in Christendom, we define **Might** as **a God-given ability** to do something; a supernatural Might.

From the above Christian definition of **Might**, you can see that we are talking about the **Might** that you cannot come up with by yourself. **For instance, by God's grace, every one of us is able to get out of bed in the morning, but to do more than that, you need God's grace of <u>strength</u>, <u>power</u> and <u>might</u>.** This is why **Ecclesiastes 6:2** says:

> "<u>A man to whom God hath given riches, wealth, and honour, so that he wanteth nothing for his soul of all that he desireth</u>, **yet God giveth him not power** (*and might*) **to eat thereof, but a stranger eateth it:** this is vanity, and it is an evil disease."

You may have the physical strength to gather wealth and riches for yourself but if God does not give you **His strength,**

power and **might** to enjoy it, a stranger will be the one to enjoy all the fruits of your labor. Power and might go hand in hand and we need them on a daily basis.

Our God is a Mighty God

The Lord Jesus needed the Anointing of **Might** in His life and as a result, it was necessary that the **Spirit of Might** should rest upon Him so that He can manifest this attribute of God. He has to demonstrate **Might** in His ministry and He did this when He single handedly drove out all the people that were buying and selling things in the Temple in Jerusalem; including the money changers — **John 2:13-16**:

> "And the Jews' Passover was at hand, and Jesus went up to Jerusalem, 14 <u>And found in the temple those that sold oxen and sheep and doves, and the changers of money sitting</u>: 15 **And when <u>he had made a scourge of small cords</u>, he drove them all out of the temple, and the sheep, and the oxen; and poured out the changers' money, and overthrew the tables**; 16 And said unto them that sold doves, Take these things hence; make not my Father's house an house of merchandise."

He also took on the devil, his evil angels, demons, sicknesses, diseases, hell death and the grave and He trampled them all in victory. He fulfilled the scripture that says that our God is a **Mighty God** in **Deuteronomy 10:17**:

> "For the LORD your God is God of gods, and Lord of lords, a great God, **a mighty,** and **a terrible,** which regardeth not persons, nor taketh reward."

And in **Deuteronomy 7:23**, it says:

> "But **the LORD thy God shall deliver them unto thee, and shall destroy them with a mighty destruction,** until they be destroyed."

God is the Giver of Might or Strength

No one can have true **Might** except it is given to them by God. Physical power and might profit very little and they have been known to get some people in trouble with the law. There are a lot of people in prison today because, they trusted in their physical power or might and got involved in a fight that resulted in someone's death. Remember what is declared about **Wisdom** in **Proverbs 8:14** which says:

> "Counsel is mine and sound wisdom: I am understanding; **I have strength.**"

Who do you think is speaking in the above scripture? God Almighty is. This is why, **true wisdom, true understanding** and **true strength** (power and might), all come from God and they dwelt in the Lord Jesus Christ. **Today, Christians get them from Him because we are one with Him and we dwell in Him.** He also told us in **John 15:4-5**, to remain attached to Him because He is the 'True Vine' and we are His branches. As a result, we need Him to be able to do anything because without Him, we can do nothing:

> "Abide in me, and I in you. **As the branch cannot bear fruit of itself, except it abide in the vine; no more can ye, except ye abide in me.** 5 I am the vine, ye are the branches: He that abideth in me, and I in him, the same bringeth forth much fruit: **for without me ye can do nothing.**"

Today, we the believers who are attached to Him, use the power of the name of the Lord Jesus to heal the sick, cast out devils and rule over principalities, powers and spiritual wickedness. We are reigning on earth in His name and with His power.

Misuse of God's Power and Might

The man **Samson** was endowed by God with the **Spirit of Power and Might** but he misused it as we see in the biblical account about his life — **Judges 13:24-25**:

"And the woman bare a son, and called his name Samson: and the child grew, and the LORD blessed him. 25 **And the Spirit of the LORD began to move him at times** in the camp of Dan between Zorah and Eshtaol."

The **Spirit of power and might** gave Samson the unusual power to single handedly kill all his enemies. For example, we read in **Judges 15:14-16**, that when the Philistines shouted against him and they rushed to kill him, the **Spirit of Might** came upon Samson and he killed a thousand men with just the jawbone of an ass:

> "And when he came unto Lehi, the Philistines shouted against him: and the **Spirit of the LORD came mightily upon him, and the cords that were upon his arms became as flax that was burnt with fire, and his bands loosed from off his hands. 15 And he found a new jawbone of an ass, and put forth his hand, and took it, and slew a thousand men therewith. 16 And Samson said, With the jawbone of an ass, heaps upon heaps, with the jaw of an ass have I slain a thousand men**."

Samson's refusal to learn from his mistakes began when he put forth **a riddle** to the lords of the Philistines on **his wedding day. The lords of the Philistines threatened his fiancé and she pleaded with Samson until her pleas wore him down. He told her the meaning of the riddle and she promptly told it to the lords of the Philistines.** As a result, on the appointed day, the lords of the Philistines were able to tell Samson the meaning of his riddle and he knew that his fiancé had betrayed him — Judges 14:19:

> "And the Spirit of the LORD came upon him, and he went down to Ashkelon, and slew thirty men of them, and took their spoil,** and gave change of garments unto them which expounded the riddle..."

You will think that Samson learned his lesson from this **betrayal** but he did not because, in the next account of his life, we see him involved again with another Philistine woman named Delilah. The lords of the Philistines <u>contracted with her for money</u> to find out the secret to Samson's power. **Just like Samson's former fiancé, she too <u>pleaded</u> with him to tell her the secret of his power and how he could be made powerless.**

   She also wore Samson down with her pleas and he told her his secret. Upon hearing it, she immediately got Samson drunk and shaved off his hair which made him powerless. **Afterwards, she called the lords of the Philistine who then took Samson and began to mock him and to make him grind in their mill like a donkey** — Judges 16:15-21:

> "And she said unto him, How canst thou say, I love thee, when thine heart is not with me? thou hast mocked me these three times, and hast not told me wherein thy great strength lieth. 16 **And it came to pass, when she pressed him daily with her words, and urged him, so that his soul was vexed unto death;**
>
> 17 **That he told her all his heart, and said unto her, There hath not come a razor upon mine head; for I have been a Nazarite unto God from my mother's womb: if I be shaven, then my strength will go from me, and I shall become weak, and be like any other man.**
>
> 18 And when Delilah saw that he had told her all his heart, <u>she sent and called for the lords of the Philistines, saying, Come up this once, for he hath shewed me all his heart</u>. Then the lords of the Philistines came up unto her, and brought money in their hand. 19 **And she made him sleep upon her knees; and she called for a man, and she caused him to shave off the seven locks of his head; and she began to afflict him, and his strength went from him.**

20 And she said, The Philistines be upon thee, Samson. <u>And he awoke out of his sleep, and said, I will go out as at other times before, and</u> **shake myself**. **And he wist not that the LORD was departed from him.** 21 But the Philistines took him, and **put out his eyes,** and brought him down to Gaza, and **bound him with fetters of brass; and he did** <u>grind</u> **in the prison house."**

Although Samson judged Israel for 20 years, he was **compromising in his character** and was also **driven by lust**. His **reckless disregard for morals, Mosaic Law** and **lust** serve as a lesson for all who are anointed by God and lack morals or self-discipline.

God's Power and Might in King David

God also gave His **Spirit of Power and Might** to David beginning from when he was a young man and **a lion** and a **bear** came against his sheep. The Spirit of God (power and might) helped him to gain victory over them both. It was also the case when he fought against Goliath the Philistine giant. Goliath had spoken against the God of Israel and he cursed David by his gods so God showed up to help David. **Therefore, when young David threw the stone at Goliath,** <u>the Holy Spirit</u> **took the stone and landed it on the forehead of Goliath; it sunk deep into his head and killed him.**

Just imagine that an ordinary teenager (though not so ordinary because he was anointed by God) could throw a stone that could sink into the <u>thick skull of a giant</u>. It has to be by the power of the **Spirit of Might**. Again, **only God gives Power and Might** as we see in this case concerning David and his victory over Goliath in **1 Samuel 17:33**:

"And Saul said to David, Thou art not able to go against this Philistine to fight with him: for thou art but a youth, and he a man of war from his youth. 34 **And David said unto Saul, Thy servant kept his father's sheep, and there came a lion, and a bear,** and took a lamb out of the flock: 35 **And I went out after him, and smote him, and delivered it out of his mouth: and when he arose against me, I caught him by his beard, and smote him, and slew him.**

36 **Thy servant slew both the lion and the bear: and this uncircumcised Philistine shall be as one of them, seeing he hath defied the armies of the living God.** 37 **David said moreover, The LORD that delivered me out of the paw of the lion, and out of the paw of the bear, he will deliver me out of the hand of this Philistine.** And Saul said unto David, Go, <u>and the LORD be with thee</u>...

40 <u>And he took his staff in his hand, and chose him five smooth stones out of the brook, and put them in a shepherd's bag which he had, even in a scrip; and his sling was in his hand: and he drew near to the Philistine.</u> 41 And the Philistine came on and drew near unto David; and the man that bare the shield went before him. 42 **And when the Philistine looked about, and saw David, he disdained him: for he was but a youth, and ruddy, and of a fair countenance.**

43 <u>And the Philistine said unto David, Am I a dog, that thou comest to me with staves?</u> **And the Philistine cursed David by his gods.** 44 And the Philistine said to David, Come to me, and I will give thy flesh unto the fowls of the air, and to the beasts of the field. 45 **Then said David to the Philistine, Thou comest to me with a sword, and with a spear, and with a shield: but I come to thee in the name of the LORD of hosts, the God of the armies of Israel, whom thou hast defied.**

46 <u>This day will the LORD deliver thee into mine hand; and I will smite thee, and take thine head from thee; and I will give the carcases of the host of the Philistines this day unto the fowls of the air, and to the</u>

wild beasts of the earth; that all the earth may know that there is a God in Israel. *47* **And all this assembly shall know that the LORD saveth not with sword and spear: for the battle is the LORD'S, and he will give you into our hands.** *48* And it came to pass, when the Philistine arose, and came and drew nigh to meet David, that David hasted, and ran toward the army to meet the Philistine.

49 **And David put his hand in his bag, and took thence a stone, and slang it, and smote the Philistine in his forehead, that the stone sunk into his forehead; and he fell upon his face to the earth.** *50* So David prevailed over the Philistine with a sling and with a stone, and smote the Philistine, and slew him; but there was no sword in the hand of David. *51* **Therefore David ran, and stood upon the Philistine, and took his sword, and drew it out of the sheath thereof, and slew him, and cut off his head therewith..."**

As you can see, God gave David the **Spirit of Might** at a very young age. Even as an adult, every time he went to battle, he won because God was with him. David acknowledged this in **2 Samuel 7:18-20**:

"Then went king David in, and sat before the LORD, and he said, **Who am I, O Lord GOD? and what is my house, that thou hast brought me hitherto**? *19* **And this was yet a small thing in thy sight, O Lord GOD; but thou hast spoken also of thy servant's house for a great while to come.** And is this the manner of man, O Lord GOD? *20* And what can David say more unto thee? for thou, Lord GOD, knowest thy servant."

As an added blessing, God told King David that He would always have a son on the throne of Israel and today, the **Lord Jesus Christ** is known as the **Son of David.** He is ruling from heaven and He will physically rule the whole earth for all eternity from the New Jerusalem when He returns to earth.

Chapter 8
Understanding the Spirit of the Fear of the Lord

The **Spirit of the Fear of the Lord** is the last Spirit that is listed as resting upon the Messiah in **Isaiah 11:2**:

> "And the spirit of the LORD shall rest upon him, the spirit of wisdom and understanding, the spirit of counsel and might, the spirit of knowledge and **Spirit of the Fear of the Lord.**"

The Definition of the Fear of the Lord

Fear is defined as the feeling induced by perceived danger or threat that occurs in certain organisms which causes a change in metabolism, organ functions and ultimately a change in behavior such as **fleeing, hiding** or just **freezing.** It is an unpleasant emotion caused by a belief that someone or something is dangerous and is likely to cause threat or pain. Fear is very real.

A lot of people spend their whole life living in this type of fear which the medical professionals call **phobia** and it comes in many forms. One of the worst fears is the type that cripples people and renders them unable to leave their homes. **The reason for this is because this type of fear is from the devil and he uses it to hold people in <u>bondage</u>.** As a result, a lot of people are afraid of many different things in life. The truth is that <u>the underlying fear of it all is, the **fear of death**</u> as we see in **Hebrews 2:14-15**:

> "<u>Forasmuch then as the children are partakers of flesh</u> and blood, he (Jesus) also himself likewise <u>took part of the same</u>; **that through death he might destroy him that had the power of death, that is, the devil;** 15 **And deliver them who <u>through fear of death were</u> all their lifetime subject to bondage.**"

The Lord Jesus came in a human form and He destroyed the devil, death, the grave and delivered us from the bondage of fear because the Bible tells us in **1 John: 4:17-19** that this type of fear has **torments**:

> "Herein is our love made perfect, that we may have boldness in the day of judgment: because as he is, so are we in this world. *18* <u>There is no fear in love;</u> <u>but perfect love casteth out fear</u>: **because fear hath torment. He that feareth is not made perfect in love.** *19* We love him, because he first loved us."

Biblical Definition of the Fear of the Lord

What is the biblical definition of the fear of the Lord? The following scriptures provide us with the answers— **Proverbs 1:7**:

> **"The fear of the LORD is the beginning of knowledge:** but fools despise wisdom and instruction."

And **Proverbs 9:10**:

> **"The fear of the LORD is the beginning of wisdom:** and the knowledge of the holy is understanding."

Also, **Proverbs 14:27**:

> **"The fear of the LORD is a fountain of life**, to depart from the snares of death."

As a result of reading the Bible, we must all fear God enough to depart from evil because if we do not, we show God that although we are reading the Bible, we are not being transformed by it—**Job 28:28**:

> "And unto man he said, **Behold, the fear of the Lord, that is wisdom;** and **to depart from evil is understanding.**"

How to Manifest the Fear of the Lord

The Lord wants to see us manifest our true knowledge of Him by displaying the fear of the Lord in our actions. This is why the following scripture is written in **Deuteronomy 10:12-13**:

"And now, Israel, what doth the LORD thy God require of thee, **but to <u>fear the LORD thy God</u>, to walk in all his ways, and to love him, and to serve the LORD thy God with all thy heart and with all thy soul,** 13 To keep the commandments of the LORD, and his statutes, which I command thee this day for thy good?"

And in **Isaiah 8:13**, it says:

"Sanctify the LORD of hosts himself; **and let him be your fear, and let him be your dread.**"

Our God is an awesome God in the sense that He is Mighty and He has all Power. He alone can judge and condemn satan, fallen angels, men and send them all to hell forever. Therefore, you must know Him and you must fear Him enough to avoid sin. If you do not fear God enough to turn from sin, then you do not have the true knowledge and God sees you as an ignorant person or a fool. Because only God can condemn a human being to hell, the Lord Jesus told us in **Matthew 10:28** to fear Him:

"And fear not them which kill the body, but are not able to kill the soul: **but rather fear him which is able to destroy both soul and body in hell.**"

As long as we walk according to the Lord's commandments, we do not have to live our lives in fear because God loves us. When we walk in disobedience, we run the risk of being condemned to hell if our actions were ungodly throughout our lifetime. We cannot claim to have any knowledge of the Lord while our actions speak rebellion to Him.

Reasons to Walk in the Fear of the Lord

In the previous chapters on **Wisdom, Knowledge** and **Understanding,** I said that **the Lord showed me that <u>when we say that we have knowledge,</u> He must see <u>the fear of the Lord</u> manifested in our actions.** As long as He does not see this, we can quote the Bible forward and backward but on His part, **He sees us as having no knowledge.**

Another reason that having the fear of the Lord is important for us is because, everything that we are going to get from God is based on our demonstration of the fear of the Lord. I now know that God watches or tests us to see whether or not we have the true knowledge of Him. Therefore, I am determined to let sound wisdom, understanding, counsel and the fear of the Lord be reflected in my actions. The world is in the appalling state of **lack of the fear of the Lord** and it is the reason that **Romans 3:10-18** says:

> "As it is written, There is none righteous, no, not one: *11* There is none that understandeth, there is none that seeketh after God. *12* They are all gone out of the way, they are together become unprofitable; there is none that doeth good, no, not one.
>
> *13* Their throat is an open sepulcher; with their tongues they have used deceit; the poison of asps is under their lips: *14* Whose mouth is full of cursing and bitterness: *15* Their feet are swift to shed blood: *16* Destruction and misery are in their ways: *17* And the way of peace have they not known: 18 **There is no fear of God before their eyes.**"

Again, the people in the world act in ungodly ways because there is no fear of God before their eyes. As for you, know therefore that every time you do something that is contrary to the Word of God, you are demonstrating that there is no fear of God in you. I knew a man who could quote everything in the Bible but much to my surprise, one day, he went to another state and shot himself in a motel room.

I could not understand how someone who was so well versed in the Bible, would do something like that until I started studying about the fear of the Lord. His action proved the point that just because someone can quote the Bible, it does not mean that they know God. **He thought he knew God but his actions said otherwise. We must all fear God and obey the commandment, "Thou shall not kill."** This is one of the reasons why **Job 28:28** says:

> "And unto man he said, **Behold, the fear of the Lord,** that is wisdom; and **to depart from evil is understanding.**"

Christians Without the Fear of the Lord

A lot of Christians do not fear God enough to change their actions even after you talk to them about their ungodly ways or lifestyles. They choose not to live according to the Word of God but according to their own will and they rationalize their actions by telling whoever tries to correct them that the Bible said that "thou shall not judge."

Many of them claim to love God and believe Jesus to be the Lord of their lives but they do not obey His Word; they choose to live as they please. **As the Lord said, obedience to the Word of God** (the fear of the Lord) **is the love for God.** Therefore, those who profess to love God without obeying His Word or fearing Him enough to stay out of sin are liars. They choose to disregard everything that the Word of God said not to do in their pursuit of fleshly pleasures.

What they do not realize is that God is the ultimate Judge and He swore by Himself that before Him every knee shall bow and acknowledge Him as God. Meaning that every single person will come before God and bow before Him. **The question is: Are you going to bow before Him now and** acknowledge Him as your Lord and Savior or wait till you are on your way to hell as you regret not doing so while you had the chance here on earth? If you wait till then, trust me, you will have all of eternity to regret your foolishness and your stupidity but then, it will be too late.

Ministers Without the Fear of the Lord

Today, it is very sad to see that some of God's ministers in the Church do not teach their members about the fear of God anymore. They also no longer preach against sin. God's message is being watered down and it is giving people false illusions about the nature of our God. It has been a long time since I heard anyone teaching about the fear of the Lord and as a result, many people do not fear God enough to stay away from sin. They think that God is like Santa Clause or just a loving father that tells His children, "Do not worry because you will be OK no matter what."

The Bible remains true that, **"without holiness, no man shall see God"** (Hebrews 12:14). **This is because God hates sin so much that at one point in human history, He destroyed all mankind but saved only Noah and his family!** Therefore, you must learn to fear God because He still does and always will require righteousness and holiness to get into His heaven. Ministers who choose to ignore this about God and are <u>not living</u> according to His Word, are going to be shocked when He bars (prevents) them from entering into His heaven. The Lord Jesus calls these ministers, "workers of iniquity" as we see in **Matthew 7:21-23**:

> **"Not everyone that saith unto me, Lord, Lord, shall enter into the kingdom of heaven;** but <u>he that doeth the will of my Father which is in heaven</u>. 22 **Many will say to me in that day, Lord, Lord, <u>have we not prophesied in thy name</u>**? and <u>in thy name have cast out devils? and in thy name done many wonderful works</u>? 23 **And then will I profess unto them, I never knew you: depart from me, ye that work iniquity."**

These are ministers and Christians who prophesized and did all types of ministries in the Lord's name. In other word, they preached and taught the Word but they were not living it. Talking about these types of people, the Lord said to me one day, "**Do you know that Judas was one of the 12? Do you know that He was one of those who went out and cast out devils?**" Yes, **Judas** was one of those who returned with great joy because "the spirits were subjected unto them." Yet, **Judas** <u>did not have the fear of the Lord</u> and as a result, he never turned his life around in obedience to the Lord's commandments.

I asked the Lord, "**Since Judas was with You for three and a half years, why did You never pull him aside and talk to him when he was stealing from the purse?**" The Lord's answer was, "**I spoke to all of them and Judas was with Me and He heard my teachings.**" We are all required to let the Word of God change us as we heard it or read it. Only the fear of the Lord can make someone stay away from sin even when no one is looking.

When you yield your life to the **Holy Spirit** and choose to live by the Word of God, He will help you to turn your life around so that if, for instance, you used to steal, He can help you to stop. He will show you that 'the pretty little things' that the devil is making to glitter before you or 'to push your button' and cause you to steal, will put you in hell. This is because, God will hold you accountable for all your actions.

On judgment day, what seemed to you on earth like nothing but before God a sin, will place you in hell if you do not repent of it. We must be willing to separate ourselves from the world and put a difference between that which is clean (righteous) and that which is unclean or unrighteous. It is why the Word of God said in **2 Corinthians 6:14-18**:

> "**Be ye not unequally yoked together with unbeliev- ers: for what fellowship hath righteousness with**

unrighteousness? and **what communion hath light with darkness**? *15* And what concord hath Christ with Belial? or **what part hath he that believeth with an infidel**? *16* And what agreement hath the temple of God with idols? for ye are the temple of the living God; as God hath said, I will dwell in them, and walk in them; and I will be their God, and they shall be my people. *17* **Wherefore come out from among them, and be ye separate, saith the Lord, and touch not the unclean thing; and I will receive you,** *18* And will be a Father unto you, and ye shall be my sons* and daughters, saith the Lord Almighty."

All those who live a life of unrighteousness by willfully committing sin while professing to be Christians will face God's judgment. Just because you go to church every Sunday or serve in the church does not exempt you from walking in the fear of the Lord by avoiding sin. We all need holiness to see God or enter heaven.

Chapter 9
The Blessings of Walking
in the Fear of the Lord

God Honored Levi through His
Great-grandson Phinehas

There is a legacy of blessings for future generations of those who walked in the fear of the Lord. We see this stated in the case of **Phinehas**; the grandson of Aaron (a **Levite**). According to God in **Malachi 2:4-5**, the <u>priesthood was given to **Levi** for a reward</u> because his great-grandson **Phinehas** walked in the fear of the Lord. Although **Levi** had been dead for hundreds of years, yet, God honored him through his great-grandson by naming the **Levitical priesthood** after him:

> "And ye shall know that I have sent this command-ment unto you, <u>that **my covenant** might be with **Levi,** saith the LORD</u> of hosts. 5 **My covenant was with him of life and peace; and <u>I gave them to him for the fear wherewith he feared me</u>, and was afraid before my name.**"

Levi was the Son of Jacob and the priesthood was not established until three generations from him. **While establishing the priesthood, God remembered this son of Jacob because his great-grandson walked in His fear**. As a result, God honored him by giving the priesthood to his great-grandchildren; He made them priests forever. **We see the genealogy of Levi through Leah** in **Genesis 29:32-34:**

> "And Leah conceived, and bare a son, and she called his name **Reuben**: for she said, Surely the LORD hath looked upon my affliction; now therefore my husband will love me. 33 And she conceived again, and bare a son; and said, Because the LORD hath heard that I was hated, he hath therefore given me this son also: and she called his name **Simeon**. 34

> And she conceived again, and bare a son; and said, Now <u>this time will my husband be joined unto me</u>, because I have born him three sons: therefore was his name called <u>Levi</u>."

Levi was the cry of Leah's heart which was to be joined to her husband but Jacob did not attach himself to Leah because he never loved her. Rachel was the love of his life. **We see Leah's desire being fulfilled by God in joining the Levites to Himself.** Also, when it came to the great-grandsons of **Levi**; Aaron and Moses, God made Moses the spokesperson and Aaron the High Priest in honor of **Levi**. He told Moses to anoint Aaron and his children for the office of the priesthood throughout their generations **–Leviticus 8:1-13**:

> "And the LORD spake unto Moses, saying, 2 Take Aaron and his sons with him, and the garments, and the anointing oil, and a bullock for the sin offering, and two rams, and a basket of unleavened bread; 3 And gather thou all the congregation together unto the door of the tabernacle of the congregation. 4 And Moses did as the LORD commanded him; and the assembly was gathered together unto the door of the tabernacle of the congregation.
>
> 5 And Moses said unto the congregation, This is the thing which the LORD commanded to be done. 6 **And Moses brought Aaron and his sons, and washed them with water. 7 And he put upon him the coat, and girded him with the girdle, and clothed him with the robe, and put the ephod upon him, and he girded him with the curious girdle of the ephod, and bound it unto him therewith.** 8 And he put the breastplate upon him: also he put in the breastplate the **Urim** and the **Thummim**.
>
> 9 **And he put the mitre upon his head; also upon the mitre, even upon his forefront, did he put the golden plate, the holy crown; as the LORD commanded**

Moses. 10 And Moses took the anointing oil, and anointed the tabernacle and all that was therein, and sanctified them. 11 And he sprinkled thereof upon the altar Seven times, and anointed the altar and all his vessels, both the laver and his foot, to sanctify them.

12 **And he poured of the anointing oil upon Aaron's head, and anointed him, to sanctify him.** 13 **And Moses brought Aaron's sons, and put coats upon them, and girded them with girdles, and put bonnets upon them; as the LORD commanded Moses."**

This **Leviticus priesthood** remained in place until the **Death, Resurrection** and **Ascension** of the **Lord Jesus**. It shows us how God honors or rewards those who walk in His fear even many generations after they are dead. He honors them still through their children, grandchildren and great-grandchildren up to a thousand generations (Exodus 20:6 ISV).

What Phinehas Did to Get the Blessing from God

The question is: **Why did Phinehas get this great blessing from God and how did he demonstrate his fear of the Lord to earn him this generational blessing from God?** The answer is that he carried out God's judgment on an idol worshipper and his foreign woman. It happened when God was in the process of pouring out His judgement upon the children of Israel because they very quickly departed from Him and began to worship the gods of the foreign women they attached themselves to.

Therefore, God poured out His judgment on the children of Israel and as a result, many people began to die in the camp. Under Moses's advice, the entire congregation of children of Israel came together to repent in order to turn away God's anger. As the people were in the midst of repenting, one of the men of the children of Israel brought his Medianite woman into the camp in the sight of Moses and all the congregation. **Upon seeing them, Phinehas went after the man and his Medianite woman and killed them both with a javelin.** His action pacified God's wrath and He blessed him and the generations after him. We read about these events in **Numbers 25:1-13**:

> "And Israel abode in Shittim, and the people began to commit whoredom with the daughters of Moab. 2 **And they called the people unto the sacrifices of their gods: and the people did eat, and bowed down to their gods. 3 And Israel joined himself unto Baalpeor: and the anger of the LORD was kindled against Israel.**
>
> 4 And the LORD said unto Moses, Take all the heads of the people, and hang them up before the LORD against the sun, that the fierce anger of the LORD may be turned away from Israel. 5 **And Moses said unto the judges of Israel, Slay ye everyone his men that were joined unto Baalpeor.** 6 And, behold, one of the children of Israel came and brought unto his brethren a Midianitish woman in the sight of Moses, and in the sight of all the congregation of the children of Israel, who were weeping before the door of the tabernacle of the congregation.
>
> 7 **And when Phinehas, the son of Eleazar, the son of Aaron the priest, saw it, he rose up from among the congregation, and took a javelin in his hand; 8 And he went after the man of Israel into the tent, and thrust both of them through, the man of Israel, and the woman through her belly. So the plague was stayed from the children of Israel.** 9 And those that died in the plague were twenty and four thousand.
>
> 10 And the LORD spake unto Moses, saying, 11 **Phinehas, the son of Eleazar, the son of Aaron the priest, hath turned my wrath away from the children of Israel, while he was zealous for my sake**

among them, that I consumed not the children of
Israel in my jealousy. *12* <u>Wherefore say, Behold,
I give unto him my covenant of peace:</u> *13* <u>And
he shall have it, and his seed after him,</u> <u>even the
covenant of an everlasting priesthood;</u> because he
was zealous for his God, and made an atonement
for the children of Israel."

As you can see, **God honored Levi** by honoring his great-
grandson called **Phinehas**. As for the leaders who disobeyed
and worshipped idols, God required all their heads to be
hung on trees. This judgment did not stop the children of
Israel from continuing to seek after idols because they did not
stop mingling with Mediante women.

It all began when <u>Balak</u> the King of Moab hired <u>Balaam</u>
(the then known Prophet) **to curse the children of Israel
for him.** Balaam was perverse because of his love of money
and greed and he tried to curse the children of Israel but
God would not let him curse them. When he found out that
he could not curse the children of Israel because they were
blessed of the Lord and that God curses anyone that curses
them, **he told King Balak how to get children of Israel to be
rejected by God.**

**Balaam advised King Balak to enourage the children
of Israel to marry his women so that they can become
involved in idolatry.** This is because Balaam knew that those
who worship idols become an abomination to God as we see
in **Isaiah 41:24**:

"Behold, ye *(idols)* are of nothing, and your work of
nought: **an abomination is he that chooseth you.**"

King Balak did as Balaam advised him and as a result, the
children of Israel became heavily involved in idolatry through
their foreign wives. From then on, the children of Israel began
to worship Baal on a daily basis and it remained a problem

between God and the children of Israel for many generations until they were carried away into captivity.

Abraham was Honored by God for His Fear of the Lord

Another person that God honored because he walked **in the fear of the Lord** was the patriarch **Abraham**. His fear of the Lord and his obedience were tested by God when God required him to sacrifice his beloved son Isaac. **Abraham was not aware that God was testing him but he obeyed God's request even though he and his wife Sarah had waited for decades to have a child.** When Sarah was 90 years old and Abraham 100 years old, God gave them a son that they called **Isaac.** You can imagine how precious this son was to them.

To make the request to sacrifice Isaac even more bizarre, God Himself had visited them and told them that they were going to have this son and now, He wants Abraham to kill him in sacrifice to Him. Since God did not tell Abraham that the request was a test, Abraham prepared to kill his well-beloved son as a sacrifice to God — **Genesis 22:1-12**:

> "And it came to pass after these things, **that God did tempt** *(tested)* **Abraham**, and said unto him, Abraham: and he said, Behold, here I am. 2 **And he said, Take now thy son, <u>thine only son Isaac, whom thou lovest</u>, and get thee into the land of Moriah; and offer him there for a burnt offering upon one of the mountains which I will tell thee of.** 3 And Abraham rose up early in the morning, and <u>saddled his ass</u>, and **took two of his young men with him,** and <u>Isaac his son</u>, and <u>clave the wood for the burnt offering</u>, and <u>rose up</u>...
>
> 9 <u>And they came to the place which God had told him of; and Abraham built an altar there, and laid the wood in order, and bound Isaac his son, and laid him on the altar upon the wood.</u> 10 **And Abraham**

stretched forth his hand, and took the knife to slay his son. *11* And the angel of the LORD called unto him out of heaven, and said, Abraham, Abraham: **and he said, Here am I.** *12* And he said, Lay not thine hand upon the lad, neither do thou anything unto him: **for now I know that thou fearest God, seeing thou hast not withheld thy son, thine only son from me."**

As a **result of his obedience,** God **blessed** Abraham and the generations after him as recorded in **Genesis 22:15-18**:

"And the angel of the LORD called unto Abraham out of heaven the second time, *16* And said, **By myself have I sworn**, saith the LORD, for because thou hast done this thing, and hast not withheld thy son, thine only son:

17 **That in blessing I will bless thee, and in multiplying I will multiply thy seed as the stars of the heaven, and as the sand which is upon the sea shore;** and thy seed shall possess the gate of his enemies; *18* And in **thy seed** shall all the nations of the earth be blessed; **because thou hast obeyed my voice.**"

He became the father of many nations and the human ancestor of the Lord Jesus Christ. Today, the **Lord Jesus** is called the **'Seed of Abraham'** through King David and everyone who comes into the Kingdom of God since **His Death and Resurrection** is also called the **'Seed of Abraham.'** Also, as a confirmation of His Word to Abraham, everyone on earth today **who receives blessings from God,** gets them through the Lord Jesus; the 'Seed of Abraham.'

The **primary blessing is Salvation;** having eternal life with God. **A lot of people might accumulate material things, riches and fame, but the Lord Jesus says that it all means nothing if they do not have God's life.** Meaning that, it is not wise to accumulate earthly wealth and perish in hell forever when you die; it is better to save your soul and be with God in heaven forever. You cannot take your earthly wealth with you out of this world — **Matthew 16:26**:

> **"For what is a man profited, if he shall gain the whole world, and lose his own soul?** or what shall a man give in exchange for his soul?"

What God is Preparing for Those that Fear Him

In **Malachi 3:16-18**, we find out that God keeps a 'Book of Remembrance' for those that fear Him:

> "Then <u>they that feared the LORD</u> **spake often one to another: and the LORD hearkened, and heard it, and a** <u>book of remembrance</u> **was written before him** <u>for them that feared the LORD</u>**, and that thought upon his name.**
>
> 17 And they shall be mine, saith the LORD of hosts, **in that day when I make up my jewels; and I will spare them, as a man spareth his own son that serveth him.** 18 Then shall ye return, and discern between the righteous and the wicked, between him that serveth God and him that serveth him not."

Therefore, when you come together with others, do not talk about what God has not done in your life and do not question the faithfulness of God. Instead, choose to talk about how good God is and choose to walk in the fear of the Lord because God will hear you and He will bless you. **Also, you should stop accusing God foolishly, judging or blaming Him for something He has not done for you. When you speak with reverence in your heart because of the fear of the Lord, you will become part of those that God spares.** Most of us can tell the difference between those who merely serve God and those who walk in the fear of the Lord. **Those who fear Him live by His Word.**

There are many in the world today who **wave** their 'government-given rights' and think that it entitles them to do whatever they want to do. They do not believe that anyone including the Word of God should tell them how to live or behave. Their actions tell you that they do not know God and that they do not have the fear of the Lord. **This is scary because they do not know that they are booked on a one way ticket to hell based on their lifestyle and their actions.**

Prayer to Repent for Not Walking in the Fear of the Lord

If you desire to repent of your past actions and lifestyle that do not demonstrate the fear of the Lord, you can pray the following prayer:

"Father God, in the name of the Lord Jesus I come to You and I repent for the times that I did not do Your will or walk in Your fear. I ask You to forgive me and help me to learn about the fear of the Lord. As from today, I choose to fear You enough to stay away from acts of sin and to control my tongue by Your grace. Help me in the name of the Lord Jesus to choose those things that please You; Amen."

Chapter 10
Ways We Should Show Our Fear of the Lord

The Importance of Reverence

The Church has moved away from the fear of the Lord and it now views God as our buddy; to the point that some Christians now call the Lord Jesus, **JC**. A lot of people have not only lost the fear of the Lord, they have lost reverence for God. I found out in a very profound way that we must approach the Lord with great reverence or our worship is not accepted. Here is my vision about it:

> *"I was going into the Holy of Holies in heaven on one of the occasions that the Lord took me there, but I did not know that* **I was not showing my reverence for the Lord**. *Of all the worship songs on earth that my spirit could have picked to sing while entering the Holy of Holies, it picked a very irreverent song that says,* **'Jesus, O Jesus…'** *When the Lord Jesus saw me,* He told me, *'Get out.' Seeing the shock on my face,* He said, *'And reenter properly' while showing me how to* **curtsy** *in reverence before Him;* He added, *'It is, the Lord Jesus.'"*

The Lord actually taught me how to bow before Him and reverently address Him as the Great King that He is! This is why I believe that some people's praise and worship do not make it past the ceiling because they lack reverence. Therefore, if during your praise and worship, you are calling the Lord by His name; **Jesus, Jesus** or **JC**, your praise and worship will not go anywhere. It is not entertainment that God wants in the Holy of Holies but reverence in prayer, praise and worship.

Lack of reverence shows that there is no fear of the Lord in the worshiper. **By not displaying reverence in your praise and worship, you are telling God that you do not know who He is. You must come before Him boldly but not irreverently because He is not your equal.** This is what He said about Himself in **Malachi 1:14**:

> "**...For I am a great King,** saith the LORD of hosts, and **my name is dreadful among the heathen**."

And in **Malachi 1:11,** He said:

> "**For from the rising of the sun even unto the going down of the same my name shall be great among the Gentiles; and in every place incense shall be offered unto my name,** and a pure offering: **for my name shall be great among the heathen,** saith the LORD of hosts."

You must know the Lord Jesus **as** the King of Kings and the Lord of Lords so that when you approach Him, you can demonstrate this knowledge. Today, when I go somewhere and I hear someone **leading worship** while **singing irreverently** by **addressing the Lord** as, 'Jesus, 'Jesus, I add **Lord Jesus** to the song. This is not being religious but recognizing authority because God hates disrespect. As for me, when I come before the Lord in praise and worship, I do not want to be turned back again because of a lack of reverence.

The Universe Trembles at God's Voice

We must always remember that all creation trembles at the sound of the voice of the God that we serve and so, we must approach Him with reverence as <u>the one Great and only God</u>. **When God opens His mouth to speak, the universe trembles and as a result, God has only spoken to His creation a few times. <u>Since the fall of Adam, He deals with us through Christ because Christ is His Word</u>.**

He talks to us in the 'cleft of the rock' because creation cannot abide His voice; it trembles in the fear of the Lord. **This is one of the reasons why we read that on the day the Lord Jesus was crucified, <u>the sun</u>, and <u>the earth</u> registered their protest at what was being done to God's Son by the children of men.** They were terrified and refused to take part in man's wickedness to God's Son — **Matthew 27:45-52:**

"**Now from the sixth hour there was <u>darkness</u>** *(lunar eclipse)* **over all the land unto the ninth hour.** 46 And about the ninth hour Jesus cried with a loud voice, saying, Eli, Eli, lama sabachthani? that is to say, My God, my God, why hast thou forsaken me?

... 50 <u>Jesus, when he had cried again with a loud voice, yielded up the ghost.</u> 51 And, behold, **the veil of the temple was rent in twain from the top to the bottom;** and **the earth did quake, and the rocks rent** *(in fear)*; 52 **And <u>the graves were opened;</u>** and many bodies of the saints which slept arose..."

Again, they reacted in 'protest' to show that they wanted no part in what was being done to God's Son because **they did not want to be judged by God just as He did when Adam sinned** in Genesis 3:17:

"...**Cursed is the ground for thy sake;** in sorrow shalt thou eat of it all the days of thy life..."

And in **Genesis 4:10-12, the <u>earth was curse again</u>** for **<u>receiving</u> Abel's blood**:

"And he said, What hast thou done? the voice of thy brother's blood crieth unto me from the ground. 11 **And now art thou cursed from <u>the earth, which hath opened her mouth to receive thy brother's blood from thy hand;</u>** 12 <u>When thou tillest the ground, it shall not henceforth yield unto thee her strength...</u>"

God prevented the earth from yielding its strength and the earth now groans for deliverance by God from the judgment He brought upon it as a result of Adam and his descendants sins. This is how powerful the God we serve is and how He can judge the elements and the earth. We must therefore, approach Him with reverence and obey His Word.

God Can Condemn One to Eternal Damnation in Hell

The eternal reason why we must fear God is called **hell.** Most of us have never seen hell but for those who have, they will tell you that God is to be feared because of hell. **If you want to get a glimpse of what hell looks like, picture someone on fire and the fire cannot be put out. At the same time, the person is being eaten up by worms that are immune to the fire and still, the person cannot die.**

It is a place of perpetual anguish with **no relief** and **no mercy** ever. **From what the Lord allowed me to see, the flames in hell come from the ground and burn the people upward and as they try to gasp for breath, another wave comes up and it goes on and on with no end in sight.** They do not have enough time to let out a full cry or scream before they are hit with another wave of flames; it is horrible. This is why the Lord Jesus said in **Luke 12:4-5:**

> "And I say unto you my friends, <u>Be not afraid of them that kill the body, and after that have no more that they can do</u>. 5 **But I will forewarn you whom ye shall fear: Fear him, which after he hath killed hath power to cast into hell;** <u>yea, I say unto you, Fear him</u>."

Before this time, the Lord Jesus was always telling His disciples, **fear not, be not afraid** but on this occasion when it comes to God the Father, He said, **fear Him.** Now, consider how long you have been alive, there are many people who have been burning in hell from before you were born and they are still burning nonstop. **God never meant for human beings to go to hell; it was meant for the devil, fallen angels and demons but those who turn their back on God, put themselves in hell for all eternity.** It is a <u>horrible place without</u> **God, His life, mercy, grace, compassion, love, kindness, fresh air** and **light** but instead filled with **torments, burning flames** and **anguish.**

If this is not enough reason for you to have a change of heart and fear God, **then, there is the** <u>Lake of Fire</u> **that is like flowing magma from a volcanic eruption but worse because it is a hot liquid of fiery flames moving in waves like the ocean.** It will get even worse for those currently burning in hell because, the Bible says that hell and those in it will be cast into the Lake of Fire. This is known as the second death — **Revelation 20:13-15:**

> "<u>And the sea gave up the dead which were in it; and death and hell delivered up the dead which were in them</u>: and they were judged every man according to their works. *14* **And <u>death</u> and <u>hell</u> were cast into the lake of fire.** This is the second death. *15* **And whosoever was not found written in the book of life was cast into the lake of fire."**

Once in hell, it does not matter who you were on earth; whether you were a king, a rich person, a famous person, a President or a Prime Minister. **When you take your last breath and you are on the other side, what you did with God's gift of His Son** (Jesus) **to you is what determines your fate for all eternity.**

Knowing How We are Made

The Bible tells us that we are a three part being; we are **spirit** beings living in a **body** and having a **soul.** In other words, <u>we are made up</u> of **spirit, soul** and **body.** <u>The spirit in us is the breath of God</u> and at death, the **spirit** goes back to God. Your **body** came out of the ground so when a person is buried, the person's <u>body returns to dust</u>; even when cremated, the ashes will return to dust.

Therefore, <u>when you are dead</u>, your soul will bear the burden of your life's experiences and actions; whether they were good or bad. The reason is because, it is in **your soul** that you have **your emotion, your mind, your thoughts, your feelings, your judgements,** etc. **It is where you <u>conceived</u> everything and as a result, it is <u>your soul</u> that will pay for**

all the evil that you did while you were living in your body here on earth. This is why the Bible says this about the **soul** in **Ezekiel 18:20:**

"The soul that sinneth, it shall die..."

If you notice, God did not say that the **spirit** or the **body** that sins shall die. **The reason is because your soul is the real you**. Many people think that their soul is a replica of their body but the truth is, it is the other way around. **When I died physically I found out that my body is a replica of my soul because when my soul came out of my body, I looked at my body on the ground but felt no connection to it!** As I examined it closely, I noticed that body has five fingers on each hand and it looked just like the 'real me' (my soul) that was looking at it.

To me, my body was like a piece of clothing that I just took off of me; I did not feel any attachment or connection to it because it was not the 'real me.' **The body on the ground was just like the shoes that we take off our feet when we do not want to wear them anymore. Since the soul is who we really are, it is the reason that God holds it accountable for all our actions on earth.** Our souls have the exact body parts that we see in our physical bodies and it is these body parts of the soul that will be punished in hell. This is why the Lord Jesus said the following in **Mark 9:43-48:**

"And if thy hand offend thee, cut it off: it is better for thee to enter into life maimed, than having two hands to go into hell, into the fire that never shall be quenched: 44 Where their worm dieth not, and the fire is not quenched. 45 **And if thy foot offend thee, cut it off: it is better for thee to enter halt into life, than having two feet to be cast into hell, into the fire that never shall be quenched:**

46 Where their worm dieth not, and the fire is not quenched. 47 **And if thine eye offend thee, pluck it**

out: it is better for thee to enter into the kingdom of God with one eye, than having two eyes to be cast into hell fire: *48* Where their worm dieth not, and the fire is not quenched."

Every single person will come before the Judgement Seat of Christ but for those of us who received Him and are covered by His blood, we will not be judged for our sins but for our faithfulness in using the gifts that the Lord gave us. Our reward will be based on our works; **what we did for God in love.** There are some Christians that never speak of their Christian faith to other people and when you talk to them about not helping to spread the 'good news' of salvation, they tell you that they keep their Christianity to themselves. They forget that they are going to give an account of their actions to God at the Judgment Seat of Christ — **2 Corinthians 5:10-11:**

> **"For we must all appear before the judgment seat of Christ;** that every one may receive the things done in his body, according to that he hath done, whether it be good or bad. 11 Knowing therefore the terror of the Lord..."

As you just read, the Word of God is telling us that there is a Day of Judgement and that there is a terror awaiting some people from the Lord. The Bible also tells us that our God is a consuming fire so, I advise you to fear Him enough to depart from evil.

According to **Isaiah 66:23-24**, God will make the people burning in hell an example to all who will live in the next age. They will be a display of what happened to those who rebelled against God's authority. **Therefore, throughout eternity, as all humanity comes to worship God every month, on their way out from His Presence, He will let them see the conditions of these people in hell:**

> **"And it shall come to pass, that from one new moon to another** *(every month)*, **and from one sabbath to**

another, **shall all flesh come to worship before me**, saith the LORD. 24 **And they shall go forth, and look upon the carcasses of the men that have transgressed against me: for their worm shall not die,** neither shall their fire be quenched; and they shall be an abhorring unto all flesh."

Knowing that God is going to throw **hell** and all those in it into the **Lake of Fire**, and <u>**open**</u> **it for all to see** in the next life, should make you run to Christ for salvation. It should also make you hate evil lest at the end, you get thrown into hell. **If you are under a minister or preacher that is telling you that you do not have to fear God, run because you do not want to be one of those people down in hell.**

Only the <u>fear of the Lord</u> can make a person depart from evil. This is what kept Joseph while he was a slave in Egypt — **Genesis 39:7-10:**

> "**And it came to pass after these things, that his master's wife cast her eyes upon Joseph; and she said, Lie with me.** 8 <u>But he refused, and said unto his master's wife, Behold, my master wotteth not what is with me in the house, and he hath committed all that he hath to my hand;</u>
>
> 9 **There is none greater in this house than I; neither hath he kept back anything from me but thee, because thou art his wife: <u>how then can I do this great wickedness, and sin against God?</u>** 10 And it came to pass, as she spake to Joseph day by day, that <u>he hearkened not unto her, to lie by her, or to be with her.</u>"

The fear of the Lord kept Joseph from sin and it can keep you too if you are willing to run to the Lord Jesus. **You cannot avoid sin by yourself; you need divine help from the Spirit of the Lord — the Holy Spirit.**

Chapter 11
God's Delayed Judgment on Acts of Sin

Sometimes, God can wait **months** or **years** before pouring out His judgment on some people for a sin that they committed. We are going to look at two people that this happened to in scriptures; Moses and David.

God's Delayed Judgments on Moses

Remember the man Moses? God sent him to Egypt to bring out the children of Israel from Egypt but on the way to Egypt, Moses got into trouble with God and the Bible says that **God tried to kill him at the Inn**. It began with God's requirement that every Hebrew male child must be circumcised on the eight day after birth but Moses married a very willful Mediante woman named Zipporah who did not believe in this. **Therefore, when Moses tried to circumcise his son on the eighth day after his birth, his wife, Zipporah said, "No; you cannot cut my child" and Moses yielded to his wife instead of to God**.

Unknown to Moses, his yielding to his wife, angered God but when Moses headed out for Egypt, **he thought that everything was alright between him and God**. Moses had spoken to God on several occasions after this incident but **He did not know that his lack of obedience to God's covenant of circumcision, was a great sin before God.** As a result, while Moses was resting at the Inn on his way to Egypt, God showed up to kill him as we see in **Exodus 4:24-26**:

> **"And it came to pass by the way in the inn, that the LORD met him, and sought to kill him.** 25 Then Zipporah took a sharp stone, and cut off the foreskin of her son, and cast it at his feet, and said, Surely a bloody husband art thou to me. 26 **So he** (*God*) **let him go:** then **she said, A bloody husband thou art, because of the circumcision."**

This is a case of God's delayed judgment and Moses never saw it coming. Also, <u>another delayed Judgment kept the same Moses from entering the 'Promised Land.'</u> He led the children of Israel for **many years** <u>after him and his brother (Aaron) disobeyed God</u> **by striking the Rock twice** instead of **speaking to it** as God Commanded. It cost them entrance into the 'Promised Land' as recorded in **Numbers 20:8-12**:

> "<u>Take the rod, and gather thou the assembly together, thou, and Aaron thy brother,</u> **and <u>speak ye unto the rock</u> before their eyes; and it shall give forth his water, and thou shalt bring forth to them water out of the rock: so thou shalt give the congregation and their beasts drink.**
>
> 9 And Moses took the rod from before the LORD, as he commanded him. 10 And Moses and Aaron gathered the congregation together before the rock, and he said unto them, <u>Hear now, ye rebels; must we fetch you water out of this rock?</u> 11 **And Moses lifted up his hand, <u>and with his rod he smote the rock twice:</u>** and the water came out abundantly, and the congregation drank, and their beasts also.
>
> 12 **And the LORD spake unto Moses and Aaron, Because ye believed me not, to sanctify me in the eyes of the children of Israel, therefore <u>ye shall not bring this congregation into the land which I have given them.</u>**"

What Moses and Aaron did not know was that the **<u>Rock is Christ</u> and that <u>He was only to be struck on the Cross once</u>** and <u>after that **we speak to Him** to get what we want from God</u>. **This is why their actions or sin was so serious before God.** Many years after the event, God did not forget what they did but He saw to it that they did not enter into the 'Promised Land' as we see in **Deuteronomy 32:48-52**:

> "And the LORD spake unto Moses that selfsame day, saying, 49 **Get thee up into this mountain**

Abarim, unto mount Nebo, which is in the land of
Moab, that is over against Jericho; and behold the
land of Canaan, which I give unto the children of
Israel for a possession:

50 **And die in the mount** whither thou goest up, and
be gathered unto thy people; as Aaron thy brother
died in mount Hor, and was gathered unto his people:
51 **Because ye trespassed against me** among the
children of Israel at the waters of Meribah-Kadesh, in
the wilderness of Zin;

because ye sanctified me not in the midst of the
children of Israel. 52 **Yet thou shalt see the land
before thee; but thou shalt not go thither unto the
land** which I give the children of Israel."

Our God is a **righteous Judge** and He does not overlook sin
or forget when we sin and do not repent. **This is why we all
need to thank Him for sacrificing His Son, our Lord Jesus
Christ for our sins because truly, only His blood can blot
out sin. God shed His blood for us** in His Son — Acts 20:28:

"Take heed therefore unto yourselves, and to all the
flock, over the which the Holy Ghost hath made you
overseers, **to feed the church of God, which he hath
purchased with his own blood**."

God's Delayed Judgment on King David

**Another case of God's delayed judgment involved
King David.** As a King, David misused his power when
he lusted and coveted **Uriah's** wife **Bathsheba** with whom
he committed adultery. When he found out that Bathsheba
was pregnant from their adultery, King David schemed
against Uriah, had Uriah killed and then took Bathsheba to
be one of his wives.

Bathsheba gave birth to a baby nine months later and
some time went by while she and King David went about

their lives as if everything was alright but God had a problem with what King David had done; he sinned. Not only did he commit adultery, he also killed Uriah and took his wife because he was the king. **King David and Bathsheba settled into their lives as husband and wife but God did not forget their sin**. In His anger against their sin, God struck the child with sickness.

Also, He told King David that He was going to judge his house, **repay his secret deed openly** and although King David pleaded with God through prayer and fasting, he did not change God's heart. **The child died while King David was on his seventh day of fasting** — 2 Samuel 12: 8-18:

> **"And I gave thee thy master's house, and thy master's wives into thy bosom, and gave thee the house of Israel and of Judah; and if that had been too little, I would moreover have given unto thee such and such things.** 9 Wherefore hast thou despised the commandment of the LORD, to do evil in his sight?
>
> **thou hast killed Uriah the Hittite with the sword, and hast taken his wife to be thy wife,** and hast slain him with the sword of the children of Ammon. 10 **Now therefore the sword shall never depart from thine house**; because thou hast despised me, and hast taken the wife of Uriah the Hittite to be thy wife.
>
> 11 **Thus saith the LORD, Behold, I will raise up evil against thee out of thine own house, and I will take thy wives before thine eyes, and give them unto thy neighbour, and he shall lie with thy wives in the sight of this sun.** 12 **For thou didst it secretly: but I will do this thing before all Israel, and before the sun…**
>
> 15 **And the LORD struck the child that Uriah's wife bare unto David, and it was very sick.** 16 David therefore besought God for the child; and David fasted, and went in, and lay all night upon the

earth...*18* **And it came to pass on the seventh day, that the child died...**"

God's judgment against King David was literally fulfilled in King David's life years later. God waited for King David's son Absalom to grow up and He brought the judgment to pass. Absalom rose up against his father the King and over threw him from the throne fulfilling God's Word of the evil that He promised to raise against King David from his own house. As we saw in an earlier chapter, Absalom was given an **evil** and **wicked counsel** by Ahithophel who was the **grandfather of Bathsheba.**

King David had secretly defiled Bathsheba while she was still married to Uriah and it must have brought shame to Ahithophel's family. His **evil counsel** to Absalom was to **openly defile his father's concubines** (wives) **at the top of King David's palace.** It also fulfilled God's judgment that, King David's wives will be defiled publicly as a punishment for secretly defiling another man's wife — **2 Samuel 16:20-22**:

"Then said Absalom to Ahithophel, Give counsel among you what we shall do. *21* **And Ahithophel said unto Absalom, Go in unto thy father's concubines, which he hath left to keep the house; and all Israel shall hear that thou art abhorred of thy father: then shall the hands of all that are with thee be strong.** *22* So they spread Absalom a tent upon the top of the house; and Absalom went in unto his father's concubines **in the sight of all Israel**."

Lessons from God's Delayed Judgments

The lessons we learn from both Moses and King David's delayed judgments from God is that you can commit an act of sin and walk away thinking that God will just forget about it without repenting; He does not. Our God is a very Holy God. What a lot of people do not know is that when a person comes before God with their sinful nature (not Born Again), the sin in them will make that person to combust (burst into flames) because God's holiness consumes sin; the person dies.

This is why God told Moses that the **place where he was** (the Tent of Meeting), **was not a place where one can see His Face and live.** Simply put, all those that are in the 'Tent of Meeting,' **are outside of Christ** (the Rock): they cannot see God. Therefore, **God promised to hide Moses in the 'cleft of the Rock'** (Christ) **while He passed by** and that after He has gone by, Moses will see His back but **not His face —** **Exodus 33:18-23:**

> **"And he said, I beseech thee, shew me thy glory** *(Your Face).* 19 And he said, I will make all my goodness pass before thee, and I will proclaim the name of the LORD before thee; and will be gracious to whom I will be gracious, and will shew mercy on whom I will shew mercy. 20 And he said, Thou canst not see my face: for **there** *(Tent of meeting)* **shall no man see me, and live**.
>
> 21 And the LORD said, Behold, there is a place by me, and thou shalt stand upon a rock: 22 And it shall come to pass, while my glory passeth by, that I will put thee in a clift of the rock, and will cover thee with my hand while I pass by: 23 And I will take away mine hand, and thou shalt see my back parts: but my face shall not be seen. "

Not being able to see God's face is really a big deal as I discussed in one of my books titled, **"Experiencing the Depths of the Holy Spirit."** Moses would have died if he had seen the Face of God because he was not **Born Again** or recreated in Christ. **This is why only those who are Born Again can get a vision of the face of God the Father; we are in Christ. When you are Born Again, you are in the** '**cleft of the Rock**' and <u>**this is the only place where you can see God's Face and live to tell about it.**</u> Otherwise, <u>if you see God's Face in any other place, you will be facing Him as your Judge</u> and if you have sins that are not covered by the Blood of Jesus, you will die.

The point I am trying to make here is that, God and Moses had years of interactions after Moses' sin. Moses got to know God but their continual interaction did not make God forget about Moses and Aaron's sin because His delayed judgment came at the end of their lives. This is why we all must learn the importance of **forgiveness**, **repentance** and **remission of sins**. John the Baptist preached this in **Mark 1:4:**

"John did baptize in the wilderness, and **preach the baptism of repentance for the remission of sins.**"

God's judgments are just because He is righteous and He will not ignore or miscarry justice. Due to the severity of His judgments, God wants everyone to repent so that no man will have to face Him for their sins. Unfortunately, some of God's children including some ministers who study the Word of God, preach it, have large churches and hold large crusades, still secretly live in sin. They never think of God's delayed judgments in their lives.

Conclusion

This book is written to help the reader **know God** by His **Seven Spirits** because these Spirits are aspects of Him that we all need to have operating in our lives. Hopefully by reading this book, you will cry to God to give you these **Seven Spirits** because only they can help you walk **effectively** with God by giving you knowledge, wisdom, understanding, counsel, might, and they are operated by the **Holy Spirit**.

God's **Seven Spirits** will also help you to walk **victoriously** over the evil spirits that are out to steal, kill and destroy you and every good thing that tries to come into your life. The Word of God calls these evil spirits principalities, powers, rulers of darkness, and spiritual wickedness in heavenly places but they are no match for the **Seven Spirits** of our God. These **Seven Spirits** will help you to see the activities of the devil through his evil spirits and they will give you wisdom and understanding about what to do. They will also endow you with the power to overcome them.

About the Author

I am a born again Christian who believes in the preservation of human life and the sanctity of marriage as defined by the Bible. I also believe in letting God set our agenda rather than us setting the agenda for Him. Below is the biographical information about me.

Biographical Information

Name: Prophetess Mary J. Ogenaarekhua, PhD (pronounced **Oge-nah-re-qua**).

Founder: Mary J. Ministries, Inc. and
To His Glory Publishing Company, Inc.

Educational Background: BA Communications-Journalism, Masters Degree in Public Administration and a PhD in Theology

Dr. Mary Justina Ogenaarekhua was born in Nigeria. She grew up in a Muslim home with her grandparents and she attended Roman Catholic elementary and high schools. The Lord miraculously raised Mary up from the dead when she took a fatal fall in her early years. Prophetess Mary is gifted with the ability to heal the sick, to interpret visions and dreams, to hear the voice of the Lord, to discern spirits and to intercede as a mighty prayer warrior. Also, she is the Lord's scribe.

Dr. Mary operates in the gift of prophecy with the ability to see into the spiritual realm. God has opened Prophetess Mary's spiritual eyes to see His desire for His people. She's a teacher of the unadulterated Word of God; a true woman of God in rare spiritual form! She holds workshops and conferences as well as teaches and preaches on many topics including **deliverance, healing, visions and dreams, spiritual discernment, understanding the power of covenants, effective** prayers, mentoring, leadership training and much more. She conducts **evangelism and outdoor crusades internationally** with thousands in attendance.

Dr. Mary Justina Ogenaarekhua is the author of the following books:

(1) Unveiling the God-Mother. This book is a biography of *Mary's death and resurrection experience* and her early years in Africa. It details the spiritual events that happened to her before she became a Christian and before she came to the United States. She also discusses some of the holidays that a lot of Christians celebrate ignorantly.

(2) Keys to Understanding Your Visions and Dreams: A Classroom Approach. In this book about visions and dreams, she uses the Word of God to instruct the body of Christ on visions and dreams. She applies the first hand revelation knowledge that she learned from the Lord Himself. This book is a must read for everyone who dreams and everyone who sees visions. It will teach you how to interpret them with the Word of God.

(3) A Teacher's Manual on Visions and Dreams. This manual is designed to teach the average person, bishops, pastors, etc., the basic principles about visions and dreams, about sources of vision and dreams, about how to identify the sources of visions and dreams and how to analyze the contents of visions and dreams. It is meant to be used along with the above textbook titled, **Keys to Understanding Your Visions and Dreams**.

(4) How to Discern and Expel Evil Spirits. This is a very powerful book for all those who are called to the healing and deliverance ministry. In it, Dr. Mary answers the questions most people have concerning evil spirits, and she teaches on the origin of evil spirits, how to discern and expel them and she answers the question, "Can a Christian have a demon?" This is a foundational resource for all those who want to walk in great spiritual discernment.

(5) A Teacher's Manual on Discerning and Expelling Evil Spirits. This is a powerful teaching guide for those who are called to the healing and deliverance ministry. It is a teacher's tool with a step by step teaching on key principles about evil spirits, the origin of evil spirits and how to identify and expel evil spirits. It is meant to be used along with the above textbook on **How to Discern and Expel Evil Spirits**.

(6) How I Heard from God: The Power of Personal Prophesy. Prophetess Mary Ogenaarekhua outlines key principles concerning personal prophecy and she lays out a blue print of what to do with your personal prophetic words. She helps the reader understand the conditions that are attached by God to every personal prophetic word. Failure to understand these conditions will keep your God-given prophetic word from coming to pass.

(7) Effective Prayers for Various Situations: Volumes I and II (2 books). In *Effective Prayers*, Prophetess Mary outlines principles on how to pray effectively concerning various life situations. It contains prayers for almost every situation that a lot of Christians battle with. Many have given testimonies about the deliverance and blessings manifested in their lives as a result of praying these prayers.

(8) Keys to Successful Mentoring Relationships. In this book, Dr. Mary outlines the dynamics involved in a mentoring relationship and the actual steps and stages of mentoring. She also highlights the pitfalls to avoid.

(9) A Workbook for Successful Mentoring. This workbook is a powerful teaching guide for all those who want to be mentored and those who desire to mentor others. It is a teacher/ student's valuable tool for teaching and practicing mentoring. It is meant to be used along with the above textbook titled, **Keys to Successful Mentoring Relationships**.

(10) Understanding the Power of Covenants. This book teaches on the power of covenants. Covenants impact our lives for good or for bad on a daily basis. It allows us to learn about how God uses covenants, how the devil uses covenants and how God wants us to use covenants so that we can receive what He has for us and avoid the devil's attempts to use negative covenants to hinder us. Negative covenants can hinder a person's progress throughout the person's life.

(11) Secrets About Writing and Publishing Your Book: What Other Publishers Will Not Tell You. This book is a powerful synopsis of what you need to know in order to write and get your book published and also how to position your book for mass marketing. It is designed to help all those who desire to write and market their books.

(12) The Agenda of the Few. This book is a call for the Church to get back to its God-given purpose for this country which is to reach all Americans for God. For too long now, the Church has been functioning as though it is only called to one political party –the Republican Party. The issues discussed in this book are meant to remind the reader that there are Ten Commandments in the Bible and that God can choose to address any of these commandments at any given time. Therefore, we must be willing to get the Church out of the Republican Party box that we have placed it in and learn to seek God's will during each presidential election. He is God of both the Republican and Democratic Parties.

(13) The Agenda of the Masses. Just like the "Agenda of the Few" that was written to the Christian Conservatives in the Republican Party, this book addresses what the Lord showed me that a lot of the Christians in the Democratic Party are doing that equally displeases Him. They have allowed a very large segment of the Church to be pulled away by "the agenda of the masses." In other words, they have bought into the ungodly doctrines, ideologies, beliefs, and political views of the masses to the point that now, their version of Christianity within the Democratic Party is essentially "anything goes." In their attempt to please the masses, they have embraced the pagan gods and have lumped their worship together with the worship of the Judeo-Christian God of the Bible.

(14) **What Tribe of Israel Am I From**. This book is designed to answer the questions of some Christians who are trying to determine the tribe of the natural Israel that they are from. The reason they want to know this is because there are some teachings going on in Christendom in which Christians are being assigned to the various tribes of Israel. This book will help anyone to determine the tribe of Israel that they are from. It is an eye opener for anyone who desires to know the truth. It also reveals how God chooses one person over another because God is not partial.

(15) **Experiencing the Depths of God the Father, Experiencing the Depths of Jesus Christ,** and **Experiencing the Depths of the Holy Spirit** (3 books). These books will help you know God in depth as well as understand the mysteries that He has coded in His Word for you. Therefore, if you want to know God in a deeper more intimate way so that you can receive all that He has for you, these are truly the books for you.

(16) **How the Jezebel Spirits Operates and the Anointing that Destroys It**. This book is intended to help the reader understand who the Jezebel spirit is, how she works and how to defeat her. **You will also learn about her origin, her tactics (through men and women) and how to arm yourself against her.** Many people wrestle with this spirit in the workplaces, in their marriages and in their inter-personal relationships. **One of the reasons for this is because the Jezebel spirit is one of the devil's most effective agents against humanity.** Some of the people who have tried to war against her have been known to fall into one or more of her many traps because they were not adequately prepared. **This book will equip you so that you are able to both discern and expel her without falling into her ways.**

(17) **How the Witchcraft Spirit Operates and the Anointing that Destroys It**. In this book, you will learn about the different

types of witchcraft in various parts of the world, their activities and their common denominators. You will also learn about the tools of the witchcraft spirit, what attracts and what repels it as well as how to identify a witchcraft assignment. It will open your eyes to know why some witches are more powerful than others and how to defeat them all. Due to today's reality of living in a global community, a lot of the witchcraft activities that were once confined to certain continents are now found in various countries all over the world. As Christians, we need to be equipped on how to identify and overcome the regional and global witchcraft activities that are operating in our lives, families, workplaces, cities, states and countries.

Dr. Mary O. lives in Atlanta and is the founder of **Mary J. Ministries** and **To His Glory Publishing Company, Inc.** She is an ordained minister with a strong Deliverance Anointing. She has appeared on Trinity Broadcasting Network and other national television programs.

About Mary J. Ministries

Mary J. Ministries was founded by Dr. Mary J. Ogenaarekhua to equip and impart the anointing of God to the Body of Christ, for the purpose of impacting the whole world. Our goal is to help men, women, old and young to build relationships through Bible Studies, Community Outreach, Prayer Support, Caring Ministries, Teaching on Visions and Dreams, Discernment/Deliverance, Evangelism, Mentoring, Fellowship and Special Events.

As an ordained minister, Prophetess Mary O. teaches, trains and activates individuals to properly operate their prophetic gifts, discernment, deliverance and ministry outreach and interpretation of visions and dreams. Teachings provided by Prophetess Mary O. are inspired by God and are balanced biblical principles for the purpose of developing a spirit of excellence, wholeness and GODLY character.

Prophetess Mary O. is committed to helping the Body of Christ and those who do not yet know the Lord Jesus as their personal Savior to understand their God-given purpose. Mary J. Ministries regularly hosts classes, seminars, conferences and crusades in this nation as well as in other countries.

Mary J. Ministries
Phone: **770-458-7947**
Website: www.maryjministries.org

About To His Glory Publishing Co.

To His Glory Publishing Company, Inc. was also founded by Dr. Mary J. Ogenaarekhua to help writers become published authors. Our goal is to help new and established writers edit, publish and market their work for a reasonable cost.

To His Glory Publishing Company, Inc. offers one of the most cost effective and stress- free ways of getting a manuscript published.

Books published by To His Glory Publishing Company will be made available in most of the major on-line bookstores like Amazon.com, Barnes & Noble.com, Books-a-million.com, etc.

Our authors receive a 50% royalty on the net sales of their books! Upon request, we submit our published books for buyers and distributors such as Wal-Mart, Family Christian Bookstores, drugstores, Publix and Kroger for review and purchase for their chains of stores.

We are a Christian organization with the sole purpose of bringing glory to the name of our Lord Jesus Christ. Therefore, we will not publish obscene or offensive materials.

To His Glory Publishing Company, Inc. reserves the right to reject any manuscript it deems obscene or offensive.

To His Glory Publishing Company, Inc.
Phone: **770-458-7947**
Website: www.tohisglorypublishing.com

TO HIS GLORY PUBLISHING COMPANY, INC.

463 Dogwood Dr. Lilburn, GA. 30047, U.S.A (770)458-7947

Order Form for Bookstores in the USA

Order Date: _____

Order Placed By: _____   By Fax: _____

Address: _____

_____

City _____ ST/ZIP _____

Phone #: _____

Email: _____

Purchase Order#: _____

Return Policy: Within 1 year but not before 90 Days.

Price	Quantity	List Price
Shipping Method:		
Media:		
UPS:		
FedEx:		
Other (Please Secify):		
Total Price:	Total Quantity:	List Price

Ship To Address: Bill to Address:

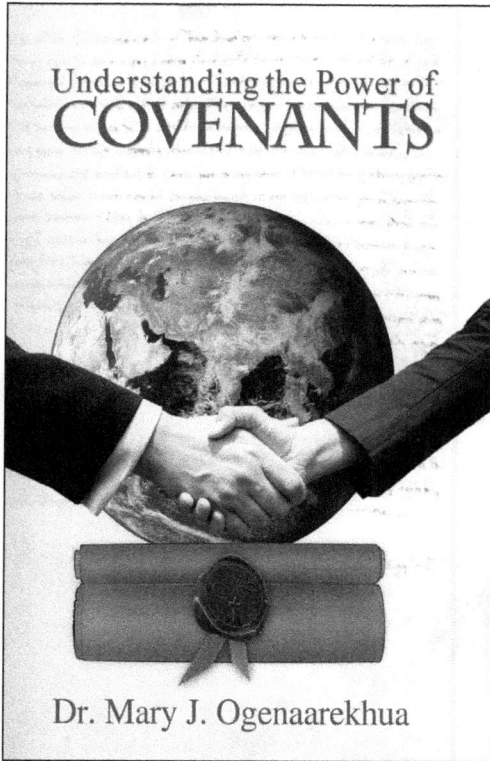

Understanding the Power of COVENANTS

Dr. Mary J. Ogenaarekhua

ISBN 978-0-9791566-8-7

ISBN 978-0-9821900-2-9

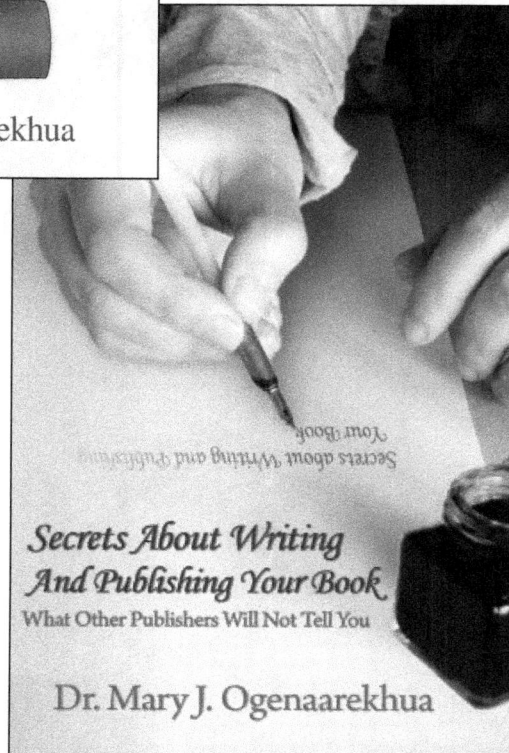

Secrets About Writing And Publishing Your Book
What Other Publishers Will Not Tell You

Dr. Mary J. Ogenaarekhua

Other Books by Prophetess Mary Ogenaarekhua

ISBN 978-1-942724-02-5

ISBN 978-0-9854992-6-6

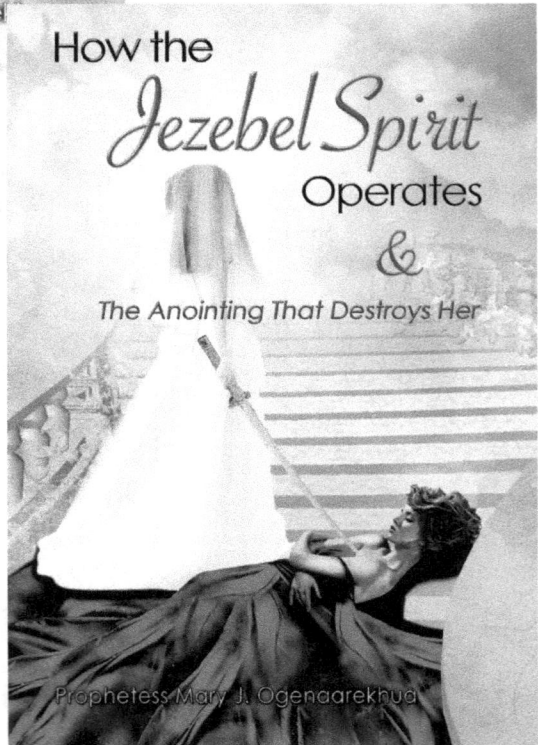

Other Books by Prophetess Mary Ogenaarekhua

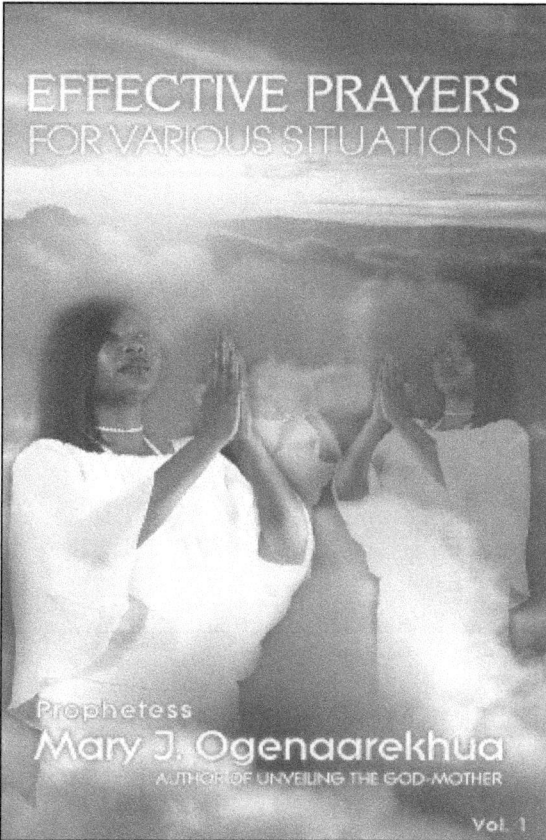

ISBN 978-0-9774265-6-0

ISBN 978-0-9774265-9-1

Other Books by Prophetess Mary Ogenaarekhua

ISBN 978-0-9749802-1-8

ISBN 978-0-9749802-8-7

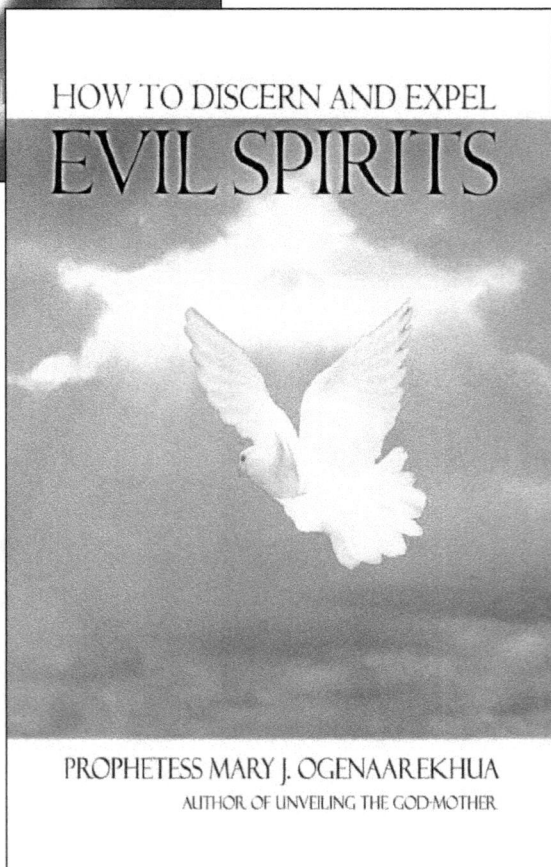

Other Books by Prophetess Mary Ogenaarekhua

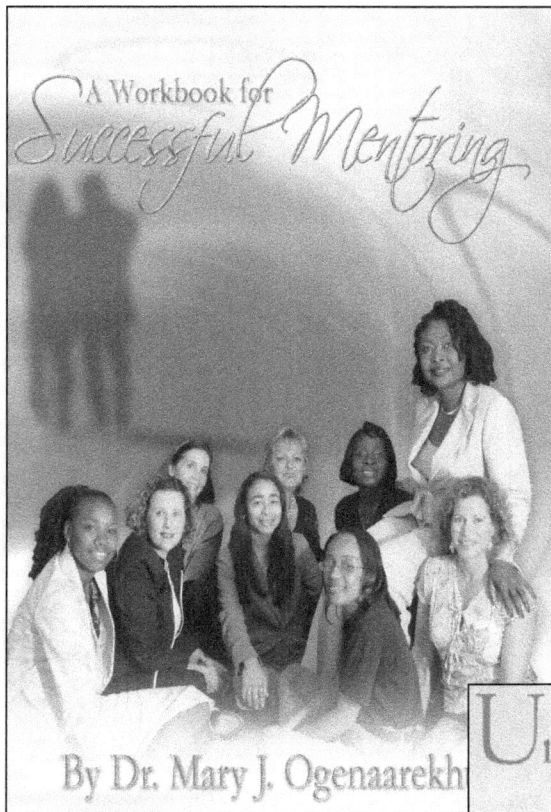

A Workbook for *Successful Mentoring*

By Dr. Mary J. Ogenaarekh[ua]

ISBN 978-0-9791566-6-3

ISBN 978-1-5873628-0-4

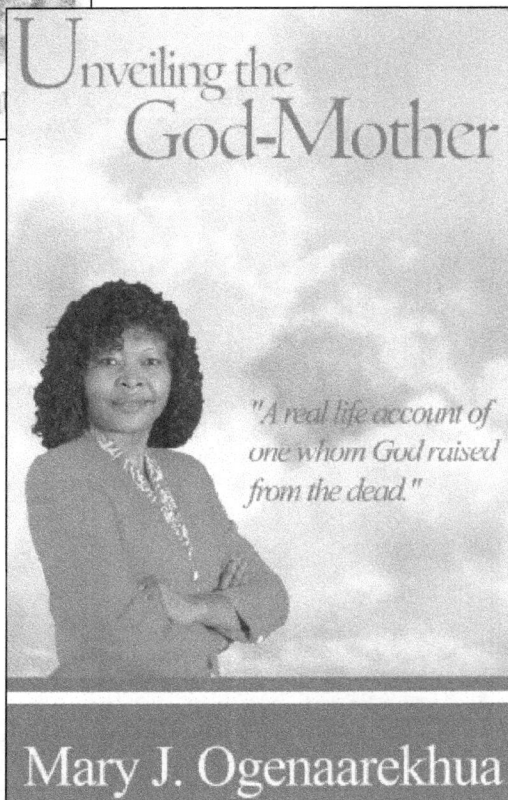

Unveiling the
God-Mother

"A real life account of one whom God raised from the dead."

Mary J. Ogenaarekhua

Other Books by Prophetess Mary Ogenaarekhua

ISBN 978-0-9821900-1-2

ISBN 978-1-5873628-0-4

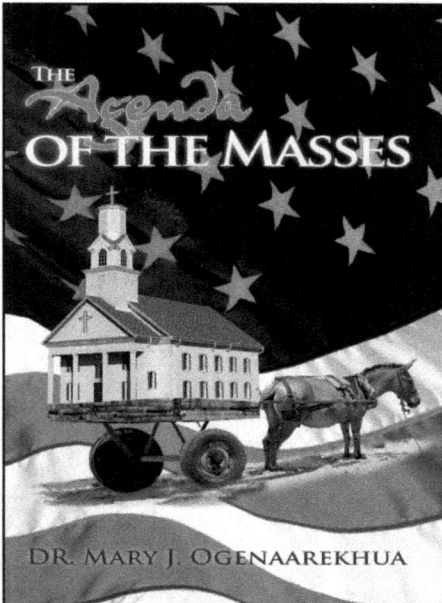

ISBN 978-0-9821900-4-3

Other Books by Prophetess Mary Ogenaarekhua

ISBN 978-0-9821900-7-4

ISBN 978-0-9854992-2-8

ISBN 978-0-9821900-8-1